MEXICAN
C·O·O·K·I·N·G

D0650883

ALLAN PUBLISHERS, INC.
1991 Edition

MEXICAN COOKING

PUBLISHED BY ARRANGEMENT WITH OTTENHEIMER PUBLISHERS INC.

Printed in Korea

Contents

Appetizers and Sauces

"Little Fat Ones"

2 cups Masa Harina	1 pound Mexican pork sausage
½ cup all-purpose flour, sifted	¼ pound Cheddar cheese, grated
½ teaspoon salt	1 small onion, chopped
1½ cups warm water	1 (4-ounce) can Green Chili Salsa
3 tablespoons melted lard	
Oil for frying	

Combine Masa Harina, flour, and salt in a mixing bowl. Add water and melted lard. Mix well; knead until well blended. Divide into 15 equal pieces. Flatten each piece into a 3-inch circle. Bake on ungreased griddle over medium heat until very slightly browned. While still warm, pinch up edges between your thumb and fingers to form a rim all around tortillas. Punch up small mounds in centers so that rounds look like small sombreros. Set aside until serving time.

At serving time, fry sausage; drain. Keep them warm.

In a small skillet, heat 2 inches oil to 375°F. Fry sombreros in deep fat until golden brown. Drain. Fill brims of sombreros with sausage; top with grated cheese and onion; drizzle with a little of the Chili Salsa. Makes 15.

Avocado Cream Dip

2 ripe avocados	Dash of paprika
¼ cup lime or lemon juice	1 cup whipping cream,
Dash of hot sauce	whipped

Cut avocados in half lengthwise, twisting gently to separate the halves. Insert a sharp knife directly into seed and twist to lift out. Peel and quarter avocados. Place in a food processor or blender container and add lime juice, hot sauce, and paprika; process until pureed.

Place in a bowl and fold in the whipped cream. Place in a serving bowl, then place on a large serving plate and garnish with tomato wedges and corn or taco chips. Makes 3 cups.

Bean Dip

1 (1-pound) can refried beans	Sour cream (optional)
⅓ cup hot jalapeño relish (or more, to taste)	¾ cup Jack cheese, grated

Combine beans with the jalapeño relish, stirring well. If mixture is too thick, add a small amount of sour cream; mix well. Place in 3 ramekins; sprinkle each with 1/4 cup of cheese. Heat ramekins, as needed, at 350°F for 20 minutes.

Serve dip hot with tortilla chips. Makes 6 servings, depending on the other appetizers.

Fiesta Cheese Ball

8 ounces cream cheese	1 tablespoon chili powder
1 pound sharp Cheddar cheese, grated	5 cups black olives, chopped
¼ cup butter, softened	½ cup dried parsley

Have cheeses and butter at room temperature before combining with an electric mixer.

Beat cream cheese and butter until combined. Add Cheddar and chili powder. Mix well. Add olives; mix lightly. Form into 2 balls; roll balls in dried parsley. Chill well. (Cheese balls may be frozen for later use.) Serve cheese balls with assorted crackers. Makes 2 balls.

Variation: omit the butter and chili powder and substitute 1 (4-ounce) can of chopped green chilies.

Avocado Cream Dip

Chick-Pea Fritters

2	cups cooked chick-peas	Dash of pepper
¼	cup onion, finely chopped	½ cup Serrano or other
¼	teaspoon garlic powder	smoked ham, diced
½	teaspoon baking powder	Olive oil for frying
1	teaspoon salt	

Mash chick-peas with masher. Add remaining ingredients except ham; mix well. Shape mixture into small balls. Press ham cube in center of each ball. Completely cover ham with dough.

Heat oil to 375°F. Deep-fat-fry balls until golden brown. Serve hot. Or heat oil in fondue pot. Arrange fritters around pot; allow guests to cook their own fritters. Makes 16 appetizers.

Chili con Queso

2 tablespoons olive oil	1 (4-ounce) can green
1 medium onion, finely	chilies, chopped
chopped	1 pound pasteurized
1 (12-ounce) can tomatoes,	processed American
drained and chopped	cheese spread

Heat oil in medium skillet; sauté onion until golden. Add tomatoes and chilies. Reduce heat to simmer; cook mixture until almost dry, stirring occasionally.

Meanwhile, melt cheese over hot water in double boiler. Combine melted cheese and tomato mixture. Serve dip in chafing dish or fondue pot, so that dip remains warm. Serve with corn chips or tostadas. Makes 6 to 8 servings.

Fried Garlic Croutons

1 (1-pound) loaf day-old	1 teaspoon garlic powder
bread	½ teaspoon salt
½ cup butter	2 tablespoons dried parsley
¼ cup olive oil	flakes

Cut bread into 1/2-inch cubes. Spread cubes evenly over cookie sheet. Let dry 2 days or until cubes lose moisture.

Heat butter and oil in large skillet until butter melts. Remove butter mixture from skillet; reserve. Add garlic powder, salt, and parsley to butter mixture; mix well.

Reheat skillet in which butter mixture was heated. Add croutons; distribute evenly over skillet surface. Pour butter mixture over croutons. Stir to distribute evenly. Fry croutons until golden brown and heated thoroughly. Cool; store up to 1 month in airtight container. Makes 2 quarts.

Mexican Guacamole

2 avocados, mashed slightly	1 tablespoon lemon juice
1 cup red onion, chopped	½ teaspoon salt
1 green chili pepper, finely	½ teaspoon pepper
chopped	1 cup tomato, chopped

Mix all ingredients together and refrigerate covered for 1-1/2 hours. Serve with corn chips. Makes about 4 cups.

Mexican Guacamole

Meat Pies

1 (10-ounce) package frozen patty shells	¼ teaspoon cumin
1 cup cooked roast beef, diced	¼ teaspoon chili powder
	2 dashes Tabasco
1 onion, chopped	1 tomato, peeled and chopped
1 clove garlic, minced	
2 tablespoons butter	¼ cup raisins
½ teaspoon salt	¼ cup stuffed green olives, sliced
¼ teaspoon pepper	
¼ teaspoon thyme	2 hard-cooked eggs, diced
	Milk

Remove patty shells from freezer and allow to stand at room temperature until soft enough to roll.

Meanwhile, prepare filling. In a small skillet, sauté beef, onion, and garlic in butter over low heat 5 minutes. Add salt, pepper, thyme, cumin, chili powder, Tabasco, and tomato. Reduce heat to simmer; cook for 10 minutes.

Soak raisins in boiling water until plump. Drain well. Combine meat mixture, raisins, olives, and eggs; set aside.

Roll each patty shell on a floured pastry cloth to a rectangle approximately 5 × 8 inches. Place 1/3 cup filling on one half of the rectangle. Fold to form a turnover. Seal with milk.

Preheat oven to 450°F. Place turnovers on an ungreased cookie sheet; brush with milk. Place in oven; immediately reduce heat to 400°F; bake for 20 to 25 minutes or until well browned and puffed. Makes 6 servings.

Shrimp Dip

¼ cup chili sauce	4 drops hot-pepper sauce
2 teaspoons lemon juice	1 cup sour cream
1 teaspoon prepared horseradish	1 (4½-ounce) can shrimp, drained and chopped (1 cup shrimp)
¼ teaspoon salt	

Combine chili sauce, lemon juice, horseradish, salt, and hot-pepper sauce. Fold in sour cream; add chopped shrimp. Chill. Serve dip with crisp vegetables. Makes 8 servings (1-3/4 cups).

Meat Pies

Nachos

1 dozen 6-inch corn tortillas	1 cup refried beans
Oil for frying	(homemade or canned)
6 pickled jalapeño peppers	½ cup sharp Cheddar cheese,
(*Jalapeño en Escabeche*)	shredded

Cut each tortilla into quarters. Heat 1 inch of oil to 360°F in a small heavy skillet. Fry tortillas until crisp; drain on paper towels.

Carefully stem and seed peppers; cut each into 6 thin strips.

Spread each chip with 1 teaspoon beans. Top with 1/2 teaspoon shredded cheese and a thin pepper strip. Broil until cheese melts. Serve immediately. Makes 48 appetizers.

Red Chili Sauce

5 dried Ancho chilies	1 clove garlic, minced
1 cup boiling water	¼ cup olive oil
1 teaspoon red chili peppers, crushed	1 teaspoon sugar
	½ teaspoon salt
1 cup canned Italian plum tomatoes, drained and cut up	⅛ teaspoon pepper
	1 tablespoon red wine vinegar
½ cup onion, chopped	

Under cold running water, remove stems from Ancho chilies. Tear each in half; remove seeds and thick veins. Tear into pieces; place into small mixing bowl. Pour boiling water over chilies; let stand 30 minutes. Drain chilies, reserving 1/4 cup liquid.

Combine chilies, reserved liquid, crushed chili, tomatoes, onion, and garlic in blender jar. Puree until smooth.

Heat oil in small skillet. Add puree; cook uncovered 5 minutes. Add sugar, salt, and pepper. Remove from heat; add vinegar. Serve sauce warm. Makes 2 cups.

Chili Salsa

2 tablespoons corn oil or light olive oil	½ teaspoon dried oregano
1 tablespoon flour	¼ teaspoon ground cumin
½ cup onion, chopped	½ teaspoon salt, or to taste
1 teaspoon garlic, finely chopped	1 cup tomato puree
	1 cup beef broth
3½ tablespoons chili powder (more or less to taste)	

Heat oil in a medium-sized, heavy skillet. Add flour and cook 3 minutes, stirring constantly. Stir in onion and garlic, cooking until onion is translucent.

Add remaining ingredients and simmer uncovered 10 minutes, stirring occasionally. Makes 2 cups.

Chilindron Sauce

¼ cup olive oil
1 clove garlic, chopped
1 onion, sliced into rings
1 green pepper, seeded and cut into strips
1 red pepper, seeded and cut into strips
Pinch of saffron
1 teaspoon salt
1 teaspoon paprika
Dash of cayenne*
1 cup Serrano or other smoked ham, diced
1 tablespoon tomato paste
1½ cups tomato sauce

Heat oil in skillet. Add garlic; fry 10 minutes. Add onion and peppers; sauté until tender. Add remaining ingredients; bring to boil. Reduce heat; simmer 15 minutes.

Use as sauce for chicken, rabbit, or lamb. Makes about 2 cups.

* If hotter sauce is desired, use more cayenne.

Garlic Mayonnaise

1 egg
½ teaspoon salt
½ teaspoon garlic powder
Dash of cayenne pepper
1 cup olive oil
3 tablespoons fresh-squeezed lemon juice

Combine egg, salt, garlic powder, and 1/4 cup oil in food processor or blender container. Blend thoroughly. With blender running, very slowly add 1/2 cup oil. Gradually add lemon juice and remaining 1/4 cup oil. Blend until thick. Occasionally scrape sides of bowl. Makes about 1 cup.

Mexican Topping

1 cup plain yogurt
2 teaspoons chopped, roasted, peeled chilies (available canned in th. Mexican food section of your supermarket)
½ cup very ripe tomatoes, diced
1 teaspoon chili powder
Garlic salt to taste
Grated Monterey Jack cheese (optional)

Combine all ingredients. Chill; serve in a small bowl. Use this to top tacos. Makes about 1-1/4 cups.

Soups and Salads

Chicken Soup with Vermicelli

6	cups chicken stock	1 large tomato, peeled,
1	whole chicken breast, split	seeded, and chopped
	(about 1 pound)	1 ripe avocado
¼	pound vermicelli	2 hot green chilies, chopped
¼	cup vegetable oil	Salt and pepper to taste

Early in the day, heat stock to boiling in large saucepan. Add chicken, reduce heat to low, and simmer for 25 minutes. Remove and cool chicken. Skin, remove from bones, and shred meat.

At dinner time, break vermicelli into 2-inch lengths. Heat oil in small skillet; lightly brown vermicelli. Drain on paper towels.

Meanwhile, heat stock again to boiling. Add vermicelli; cook until tender. Add tomato and chicken shreds; heat through. Peel and seed avocado; cut into chunks. Add avocado, chilies, salt, and pepper. Heat through. Serve soup hot with tostados. Makes 6 servings.

Hominy Soup

3	pigs feet, split, or 2 large, fresh pork hocks	1	tablespoon salt
1	stewing chicken (about 4 pounds), cut up	4	red chili pods
1	pound lean pork (Boston butt), cut up	1	(29-ounce) can white hominy, drained
2	medium onions, finely chopped		*Garnish*
2	cloves garlic, chopped	1	cup radishes, sliced
3	quarts water	1	cup lettuce, shredded
		½	cup green onions, sliced
		½	cup Jack cheese, shredded

In large kettle, combine pigs feet or pork hocks, chicken, pork, onions, garlic, water, salt, and chili pods. Bring to a boil; reduce heat to low. Cook for 2 hours. Add hominy; continue cooking until meat starts to fall off bone (3 to 3-1/2 hours total cooking time). Remove meat from broth; cool meat and broth in refrigerator several hours or overnight.

Discard chili pods; remove meat from bones. Skim fat from surface of broth. At serving time, add meat to broth; heat.

Serve soup hot in soup bowls with hot tortillas. Pass the garnishes in separate bowls, so that each diner can garnish his plate to his own taste. Makes 8 to 10 servings.

Cream of Corn Soup

3	tablespoons butter	¼	teaspoon mace
1	onion, chopped	1	chicken bouillon cube
1	medium potato, finely sliced	4 to 6	spoons heavy cream
1½	cups fresh or canned corn	1	tablespoon chopped chives or parsley (or sprinkling of paprika)
3½	cups milk		Fried Garlic Croutons (see Index)
1	bay leaf		
3 or 4	sprigs parsley		
	Salt and pepper		

Melt butter. Cook onion and potato gently, 5 minutes; shake pan occasionally to prevent sticking. Add 1 cup corn; stir well. Add milk, bay leaf, parsley, salt, pepper, and mace; bring to simmer. Add bouillon cube; cook until vegetables are tender.

Put vegetables into electric blender; blend until smooth. Or put through fine food mill. Return to pan with remaining corn (if fresh, simmer in salted water until tender.) Reheat until nearly boiling; adjust seasoning.

Serve in soup cups with spoonful of cream, sprinkling of chives, and croutons in each cup. Makes 4 to 6 servings.

Cream of Corn Soup

Corn Soup

4 cups fresh corn, cut from the cob	½ teaspoon salt
1 cup chicken stock	3 tablespoons green chilies, chopped
¼ cup butter	6 tablespoons sour cream
½ cup green onions, chopped	Tostadas
3½ cups milk	Chopped parsley

Combine corn and chicken stock in blender; blend to a smooth puree. Melt butter in large saucepan. Wilt green onions in butter. Add corn puree; simmer for 5 minutes or until thickened. Add milk and salt; cook 15 minutes over low heat.

Divide chilies among 6 soup bowls. Pour soup into bowls. Garnish each with a tablespoon of sour cream, a few tostadas, and a little chopped parsley. Serve. Makes 6 servings.

Mexican Soup

1	clove garlic, peeled	¼	teaspoon crumbled thyme
¾	teaspoon salt	2	sweet red peppers, cleaned, seeded, and chopped
4	tablespoons butter		
1	medium onion, chopped		
1	fresh hot green pepper, chopped	3	tablespoons tomato paste
½	pound baked ham, chopped	1	(16½-ounce) can whole-kernel corn
1	cup unpeeled zucchini squash, chopped	Salt and pepper	
		2	tablespoons fresh parsley, chopped
4½	cups beef broth		

On a cutting board, sprinkle garlic clove with 3/4 teaspoon salt; mash with blade of a knife.

Melt butter in a Dutch oven; add garlic, onion, hot pepper, ham, and zucchini. Sauté over moderate heat for 10 minutes. Add beef broth and thyme; simmer for 15 minutes. Add sweet peppers, tomato paste, and corn (along with the liquid from the can); stir well. Cook for 15 minutes more. Season to taste with salt and pepper.

Garnish soup with parsley. Makes 4 to 6 servings.

Note: If fresh hot peppers are not available, substitute 1 canned green chili, chopped, for the hot pepper. Three canned pimientos (chopped) may be substituted for the red peppers if necessary, but first check the frozen-foods section of your local market. Frozen chopped red peppers are now available all year round in some places.

Spanish Stew

2	pounds beef shanks	3	zucchini, sliced
3	quarts water	3	cups fresh green beans, nipped and cut into 1-inch lengths
2	cloves garlic, peeled and chopped		
1	onion, sliced	2	medium potatoes, peeled and sliced
1	tablespoon salt		
8	peppercorns	3	ears of corn, cut into 1-inch pieces
6	tablespoons tomato puree		
3	medium carrots, peeled and sliced		

Brown beef shanks in a roasting pan in a 450°F oven.

In a large soup pot, combine browned beef, pan drippings, water, garlic, onion, salt, and peppercorns. Bring to a boil, reduce heat to low, cover, and cook 2-1/2 hours or until meat is very tender. Remove meat.

Artichokes with Cold Corn Salad

Strain broth and return it to kettle. Add tomato puree; bring to a boil. Add vegetables. Reduce heat to low; cook, covered, 30 to 45 minutes or until vegetables are tender. Cut meat from bones; add to soup. Heat through. Serve stew with your favorite chili sauce. Makes 6 to 8 servings.

Artichokes with Cold Corn Salad

2 (10-ounce) packages
   frozen whole-kernel corn
⅔ cup green sweet pepper,
   chopped
¾ cup cooked carrots, sliced
2 tablespoons onion, finely
   chopped
½ cup mayonnaise
1 teaspoon chili powder
⅛ teaspoon seasoned salt

⅛ teaspoon freshly ground
   pepper
6 fresh artichokes

Chili Mayonnaise
1 cup mayonnaise
1 teaspoon chili powder
½ teaspoon seasoned salt
Dash of freshly ground pepper
1 tablespoon lemon juice

Cook corn, drain, and cool. Place in large bowl. Add green pepper, carrots, onion, mayonnaise, chili powder, salt, and pepper. Mix well; chill.

Remove artichoke stems; cut about 1/2-inch from tips of leaves with kitchen shears. Drop into boiling salted water; cook 5 minutes. Drain; shake to remove water and cool. Tap base on flat surface to spread leaves; chill. Fill with corn salad; place on serving platter.

Make chili mayonnaise. Place all ingredients in small bowl. Mix until blended; chill. Serve with the corn salad. Makes 6 servings.

Marinated Beef Salad

Salad
3 cups cooked lean beef,
   cubed
½ cup onion, chopped
2 tablespoons parsley,
   chopped
1 sweet red pepper, seeded
   and chopped
1 medium tomato, chopped

Salad Dressing
½ cup olive oil

¼ cup wine vinegar
½ teaspoon salt
¼ teaspoon pepper
½ teaspoon oregano,
   crumbled
½ teaspoon prepared mustard

Garnish
1 head Boston lettuce
1 large tomato, cut in
   wedges

Combine beef, onion, parsley, red pepper, and tomato, tossing well. Combine olive oil, vinegar, salt, pepper, oregano, and mustard; pour over salad, tossing well. Refrigerate at least 3 hours.

At serving time, line serving dish with lettuce leaves, fill with salad, and garnish with tomato wedges. Serve with plenty of crusty bread. Makes 4 servings.

Marinated Beef Salad

Fresh-Fruit Salad

1	**fresh pineapple**
2	**oranges**
½	**Spanish melon**
1	**pound green seedless**
	grapes
2	**Delicious apples**

Honey Dressing
¾	**cup mayonnaise**
⅓	**cup honey**
¼	**cup orange juice**
⅛	**teaspoon onion, grated**

Peel pineapple. Cut into 3/4-inch slices; remove rind and eyes. Cut into cubes, discarding center core. Peel and section oranges. Remove seeds from melon; slice into wedges. Wash grapes; remove from stems. Slice in half. Peel and dice apples.

Gently mix fruit in large bowl. Combine honey dressing ingredients. Serve salad with honey dressing on the side. Makes 8 to 10 servings.

Pickled Corn Salad

½ cup onion, chopped
½ cup green pepper, diced
4 tablespoons pimiento, chopped
3 tablespoons sugar
¾ teaspoon salt
½ teaspoon celery salt
½ teaspoon dry mustard
½ cup cider vinegar
½ cup water
3 cups frozen whole-kernel corn

Combine all ingredients except frozen corn; bring to a boil. Lower heat, cover pan, and simmer for 12 minutes, stirring occasionally. Add frozen corn; raise heat. When boiling resumes, lower heat; simmer until corn is just tender (2 or 3 minutes). Drain.

Serve salad hot, or refrigerate and serve on lettuce leaves. Makes 4 to 6 servings.

Cumin Salad

2 medium tomatoes, diced
½ cup onion, chopped
½ cup ripe olives, sliced
¼ cup fresh parsley, chopped
2 cups iceberg lettuce, sliced

Salad Dressing
¼ cup olive oil
2 tablespoons lemon juice
Salt and pepper to taste
½ teaspoon ground cumin
1 teaspoon dried sage leaves, crumbled
⅛ teaspoon garlic salt

Layer tomatoes, onion, olives, parsley, and lettuce in salad bowl.

Combine olive oil, lemon juice, salt and pepper, cumin, sage, and garlic salt, mixing well. Pour over salad. Refrigerate 1 hour before serving. Makes 4 servings.

Melon Salad

1 Spanish melon
1 cup fresh strawberries
1 orange
2 tablespoons honey
½ cup whipped cream
Pistachio nuts

Slice 1/4 of top off melon; remove seeds. Scoop meat from melon, using melon-ball scoop; save melon shell. Place balls in large bowl.

Wash and remove stems from strawberries. Add to melon balls. Peel orange; slice into sections by cutting between membranes. Add to melon balls. Drizzle honey over fruit. Toss gently.

Fill melon shell with honeyed fruit. Garnish with whipped cream and pistachio nuts; chill. Makes 4 to 6 servings.

Fresh Fruit Salad

Mixed Green Salad

- 1 head Bibb lettuce (or ½ head iceberg lettuce)
- 2 green peppers, cleaned, seeded, and cut into strips
- 4 small tomatoes, sliced
- 2 small onions, sliced and separated into rings
- 2 hard-cooked eggs, sliced
- ½ cup stuffed green olives, sliced
- ½ medium cucumber, peeled, seeded, and cut into chunks

Salad Dressing
- 4 tablespoons olive oil
- 3 tablespoons tarragon vinegar
- ½ teaspoon salt
- ¼ teaspoon freshly ground pepper
- 1 clove garlic, crushed
- ¼ teaspoon crushed oregano
- 1 tablespoon fresh parsley, chopped

Wash lettuce; clean, dry, and tear into bite-sized pieces. Place in salad bowl; add peppers, tomatoes, onions, eggs, olives, and cucumber. Refrigerate.

Combine all dressing ingredients; mix well. At serving time toss salad at the table with prepared dressing. Makes 4 servings.

Garbanzo Bean Salad

1	(15-ounce) can garbanzo beans, drained
¼	teaspoon garlic powder
2	tablespoons olive oil
2	tablespoons tarragon vinegar
¾	cup celery, chopped
½	cup pitted green olives, sliced
¼	cup pimientos, chopped
3	scallions, chopped
½	teaspoon salt
	Dash of pepper

Combine ingredients; mix well. Cover; marinate 24 hours in refrigerator. Serve salad in lettuce cups. Makes 4 servings.

Red Sweet Pepper Salad

6	large red sweet peppers
1	cup brown rice
1	(3-ounce) package cream cheese
2	tablespoons minced green onion
¼	cup dressing (see below)
	Salt and freshly ground pepper to taste
6	small thin onion rings
6	green stuffed olives
2	tablespoons minced chives
1	head lettuce
18	whole black olives

Cut tops from peppers; remove seeds and membranes. Rinse; invert on paper towels to drain.

Cook rice according to package instructions. Dice cream cheese. Combine with rice in large bowl; toss lightly. Fold in green onion, dressing, salt, and pepper. Spoon into pepper shells; place onion ring on top of each. Place green olive in center of each onion ring. Sprinkle with chives; chill until ready to serve. Arrange on beds of lettuce; garnish each serving with 3 ripe olives. Makes 6 servings.

Dressing: Combine 2 teaspoons salt, 1/2 teaspoon freshly ground pepper, 1 teaspoon prepared mustard, 1 cup olive oil, 1/4 cup red-wine vinegar, 1/2 tablespoon chopped onion, 1/2 tablespoon parsley, 1/2 tablespoon chopped tarragon, and 1/2 tablespoon chopped chives in a medium-sized bowl; blend well with wooden spoon. Store in covered jar in refrigerator. Shake well before using. Makes 1-1/3 cups.

Melon Salad

Pepper Salad

2 medium green sweet peppers	½ cup olive oil
3 large firm ripe tomatoes	1 to 2 tablespoons red-wine vinegar
Salt and freshly ground pepper to taste	1½ teaspoons chives, chopped
	1½ teaspoons parsley, chopped

Cut peppers in half; remove seeds and membrane. Cut into thin lengthwise slices. Slice tomatoes thinly. Arrange tomatoes and peppers in serving dish; sprinkle with salt and pepper.

Pour oil evenly over all. Sprinkle vinegar, chives, and parsley over top Makes about 4 servings.

Eggs and Cheese

Ranch-Style Eggs

Sauce

2   tablespoons olive oil
¼   cup onion, chopped
1   clove garlic, minced
1   (1-pound) can tomatoes
2   tablespoons butter
2   tablespoons green chilies, chopped

½   teaspoon dried cilantro
½   teaspoon salt

Oil for frying
4   tortillas
8   eggs
1   small ripe avocado

First prepare sauce. Heat oil in small skillet; sauté onion and garlic until lightly browned. Add tomatoes, green chilies, cilantro, and salt; simmer until thick. Keep sauce warm while cooking eggs.

Heat 1 inch vegetable oil in small cast-iron skillet over moderate heat. Soft-fry tortillas 1 at a time until they are just beginning to crisp. Drain and keep them warm.

Melt butter in heavy skillet; fry eggs sunny-side-up to desired degree of doneness. Put a tortilla on each plate. Top with 2 eggs and some of the sauce. Peel and slice the avocado; garnish the eggs with it. Makes 4 servings.

Mixed Green Salad

Eggs with Avocado Sauce

8	eggs, hard-boiled and peeled	½	cup milk
2	tablespoons butter	2	ripe avocados
2	tablespoons onion, minced	½	teaspoon salt
1	tablespoon flour	2	tomatoes, cut in wedges
1	tablespoon green chili, minced		

Keep eggs warm by placing them in hot water while preparing sauce. Melt butter; cook onion until limp. Add flour; cook until bubbly. Add green chili and mix well. Add milk; cook, stirring constantly, until thickened. Puree avocados in blender; add with salt to sauce.

Drain and halve eggs. Place 4 egg halves on each serving plate, top with some of the sauce, and garnish with tomatoes. Makes 4 servings.

Cheese Enchiladas

8 6-inch corn tortillas	*Red Chili Sauce*
Oil for frying	½ cup onion, chopped
2½ cups sharp Cheddar cheese, grated	1 clove garlic, minced
¾ cup onion, chopped	3 cups canned Italian plum tomatoes, drained
1 (6-ounce) can ripe olives, drained and chopped	½ teaspoon salt
1 recipe Red Chili Sauce (see below) or 2 (10-ounce) cans Enchilada Sauce	½ teaspoon oregano
	2 tablespoons vegetable oil
	3 tablespoons flour
1 cup Monterey Jack cheese, grated	3 tablespoons chili powder
Ripe olives	1 cup water

Soften tortillas in hot oil in small skillet until pliable (not crisp). Combine cheese, onion, and olives; toss well to combine. Place heaping 1/2 cup cheese mixture in center of each tortilla; roll up to form a tubular shape. Place enchiladas side by side in ovenproof 13 × 9 × 2-inch pan.

Top with red chili sauce or enchilada sauce. **To make red chili sauce,** combine onion, garlic, tomatoes, salt, and oregano in jar of electric blender. Whirl until smooth. Heat vegetable oil in small skillet. Add tomato mixture; simmer 20 minutes. Combine flour and chili powder in large saucepan; add enough water to make a smooth paste. Slowly stir in cooked tomato puree and 1 cup water; combine well. Cook over moderate heat, stirring constantly, until thickened. Reduce heat to low; simmer 20 minutes.

Sprinkle enchiladas with Jack cheese; garnish with additional black olives. Bake, uncovered, at 350°F for 30 minutes or until hot and bubbly. Makes 4 servings.

Mexican Scrambled Eggs

8 eggs	1 tablespoon parsley, chopped
2 tablespoons milk	
1 large tomato, peeled, seeded, and chopped	3 tablespoons butter
	½ cup ham, chopped
1 tablespoon green pepper, chopped	2 tablespoons chives, chopped

Beat eggs in mixing bowl with milk. Add tomato, green pepper, and parsley; stir well to combine.

Melt butter over low heat in large, heavy skillet; sauté ham 3 minutes. Pour in egg mixture; cook, stirring frequently with a spatula, until set. Sprinkle eggs with chives and serve with hot, buttered tortillas for brunch. Makes 4 servings.

Pepper Salad

Eggs with Sofrito

½ cup olive oil	Dash of hot sauce
1 onion, peeled and chopped	6 eggs
1 garlic clove, peeled and minced	¼ cup Swiss cheese, grated
1 cup green pepper, diced	¼ cup pimiento-stuffed Spanish olives, sliced
2 large tomatoes, peeled, seeded, and chopped	

Heat 1/4 cup oil. Add onion, garlic, and pepper; sauté until tender. Add tomatoes; cook until mixture thickens. Stir in hot sauce.

Heat remaining 1/4 cup oil in large shallow skillet. Crack eggs into skillet one at a time. Fry until whites set. Sprinkle with cheese. Cover; fry 2 minutes. Put eggs on serving platter. Garnish with sofrito and olives. Makes 4 to 6 servings.

Stuffed Chili with Cheese Casserole

	Sauce
1 (4-ounce) can California green roasted chilies (or 4 roasted, peeled Poblano chilies)	½ cup onion, finely chopped
	1 clove garlic, minced
	1 tablespoon olive oil
¼ pound sharp Cheddar cheese, sliced	2 tablespoons tomato paste
4 eggs, separated	1 cup canned peeled tomatoes, chopped
4 teaspoons flour	1 can chicken broth, regular strength
4 teaspoons water	
1 teaspoon Beau Monde	1 teaspoon sugar
¼ teaspoon salt	½ teaspoon salt
	1 teaspoon vinegar
	1 tablespoon flour
	1 tablespoon water

Lightly oil a 1-1/2- to 2-quart glass or ceramic casserole; set aside. Rinse and seed chilies. Fill chilies with cheese slices, folding and cutting cheese so that chili pepper completely encases cheese. Place in a single layer in bottom of oiled casserole.

Combine egg yolks, flour, water, and Beau Monde in a small mixing bowl; beat on low speed until well blended.

In another small mixing bowl, beat egg whites until foamy. Sprinkle with salt; continue beating until stiff but not dry. Fold egg-yolk mixture lightly but thoroughly into stiffly beaten egg whites. Pour batter over chilies; bake at 325°F for 40 minutes or until puffed and lightly browned.

Red Sweet Pepper Salad

Serve with heated stewed tomatoes with onion and green pepper or with tomato sauce. To make sauce, sauté onion and garlic in oil in small saucepan until lightly browned. Add tomato paste and chopped tomatoes; stir well. Add broth, sugar, salt, and vinegar. Cook on very low heat 1 to 1-1/2 hours or until tomatoes are soft. Force through a sieve or whirl in blender until smooth. Return to saucepan and heat until almost boiling. Combine flour and water to form a smooth paste. Slowly stir flour paste into tomato mixture. Simmer until thickened. Makes 4 servings.

Spanish Omelet

Sauce

2 tablespoons olive oil
1 small onion, chopped
1 clove garlic, peeled and chopped
2 green peppers, cleaned, seeded, and cut into strips
1 red pepper, cleaned, seeded, and cut into strips

1 (8-ounce) can tomato sauce
2 tablespoons dry sherry
½ teaspoon chili powder

Omelets

2 tablespoons butter
6 eggs

First make sauce. Heat oil in saucepan or skillet. Add onion, garlic, and peppers; cook until wilted. Add tomato sauce, sherry, and chili powder; keep sauce warm while making omelets.

In 8-inch skillet or omelet pan, heat 1 tablespoon butter over medium heat until it starts to brown. Tilt pan in all directions to coat with butter. Meanwhile, beat 3 eggs with a fork until yolks and whites are well blended. Pour into skillet; cook over medium heat until set. Fold omelet, place on warm serving dish, and repeat procedure with remaining eggs and butter.

Serve topped with the sauce. Makes 4 to 6 servings.

Mexican Fondue

1 pound (4 cups) Cheddar cheese, shredded
1 pound (4 cups) Monterey Jack cheese, shredded
¼ cup all-purpose flour
2 teaspoons chili powder
1 clove garlic, halved
1 (12-ounce) can beer
1 (4-ounce) can hot green chili peppers, seeded and chopped

Amounts as desired:
French bread, cubed
Cooked ham, cubed
Cooked shrimp, peeled
Cherry tomatoes
Green pepper strips
Avocado slices

Combine cheeses with flour and chili powder in large bowl until well blended. Rub garlic half along inside of ceramic fondue pot; add beer and heat slowly, just until beer begins to bubble. Gradually add cheese mixture, a handful at a time, stirring constantly, until cheese has melted and is smooth; add hot peppers. Serve fondue warm.

Select desired dippers and arrange tray around fondue pot. Makes 8 servings.

Mexican Scrambled Eggs

Main Courses

Boiled Beef

2	cups navy beans or chickpeas	4	carrots
¼	cup olive oil	4	parsnips
4	chicken backs, necks, and wings	4	potatoes
		1	tablespoon salt
1	(3-pound) chuck roast	2 to 3	peppercorns
2 to 3	cups water	1	bay leaf
2	onions		Fried Garlic Croutons (see Index)

Cover beans with water. Soak overnight; drain. Heat oil in large Dutch oven. Add chicken and roast; fry until browned. Add beans. Add enough water to cover meat and beans; heat to boiling. Reduce heat to simmer; cook 2-1/2 to 3 hours.

While meat and beans are simmering, clean and slice vegetables. Add vegetables and spices to stew. Simmer 1 to 2 hours or until meat is tender and falls apart when touched.

To serve, ladle broth into soup bowls; serve with croutons. Next serve vegetables. As the finale, serve the meat with Garlic Mayonnaise (see Index). Makes 6 to 8 servings.

Eggs with Sofrito

Chili Con Carne

1 **pound chuck**	2 **tablespoons chili powder**
1 **large onion, chopped**	1 **teaspoon oregano**
2 **cloves garlic, minced**	¼ **teaspoon cumin**
3 **tablespoons bacon drippings**	1 **bay leaf, crushed**
1½ **teaspoons salt**	2½ **cups canned tomatoes**
	2½ **cups red kidney beans**

Have beef coarsely ground or chop it fine. Heat oven to 325°F. Brown meat, onion, and garlic in drippings. Sprinkle with seasonings. Combine with tomatoes and turn into 2-quart greased casserole. Cover and bake for 1-1/2 hours. Remove from oven.

Stir in heated beans. Replace cover and continue baking for 20 minutes. Makes 6 servings.

Stuffed Chilies

2 medium onions, chopped	½ teaspoon pepper
1 clove garlic, crushed	4 tablespoons sliced
2 tablespoons oil	almonds
½ pound ground beef	4 tablespoons raisins
½ pound ground pork	8 whole canned chilies
1 cup fresh tomatoes,	4 eggs
chopped	½ cup flour
1 teaspoon salt	Oil for frying

Sauté onions and garlic in 2 tablespoons oil until onion is transparent. Add ground meats; stir until meat is crumbly. Add chopped tomatoes, seasonings, almonds, and raisins. Simmer.

Remove chili seeds, leaving chili skins whole. Stuff chilies with meat filling; roll them well in flour. Then dip them in the following egg batter: Beat egg whites until stiff; beat egg yolks; combine egg yolks with egg whites.

Fry chilies in deep fat at 375°F until golden brown. Remove; drain on paper towels. Makes 8 servings.

Chimichangas

4 Flour Tortillas (see Index)	1 cup blanched almonds, coarsely chopped
Chicken-Almond Filling	
2 tablespoons butter or	**Topping**
margarine	6 romaine lettuce leaves,
2 tablespoons flour	sliced
½ teaspoon salt	1 cup radishes, sliced
1 cup milk	2 ounces Muenster or
8 ounces cooked chicken	Monterey Jack cheese,
(2 cups), coarsely chopped	shredded

Combine butter, flour, and salt in a saucepan over moderate heat. Stir in milk and heat and stir until thick. Add chicken; heat through. Stir in chopped almonds. At once, spoon chicken mixture into center of each of the flour tortillas. Top with lettuce, radishes, and cheese. Wrap tortilla around filling. Serve immediately.

Tostados or taco shells may be used in place of flour tortillas, if you wish. Makes 4 servings.

Crisp-Fried Burritos

4 **large flour tortillas (7 to 8 inches in diameter or larger)**	**Oil for frying**
	Chili con Carne (see Index)
2 **cups extra-sharp Cheddar cheese, grated**	**Chopped white onion**
	Grated Cheddar cheese
1 **(4-ounce) can green chilies, chopped**	

Lay tortillas briefly on a hot griddle, to make them pliable. Fill immediately with 1/2 cup cheese and 1 tablespoon chilies placed in center of each tortilla. Fold top and bottom edges in toward center 1 or 2 inches, then fold sides toward center, overlapping each other to form a tight package. Fasten with a toothpick.

Heat 1 inch of oil to 360°F in an electric skillet. Fry burritos until golden brown, turning once. Drain on paper towels.

Serve burritos topped with chili, onions, and grated cheese. Makes 4 servings.

Spanish Omelet

American Enchiladas

Cornmeal Crêpes
¾ cup flour
½ cup cornmeal
1¼ cups buttermilk
¼ teaspoon baking soda
3 eggs
1 tablespoon butter, melted

Tomato wedges and parsley for garnish

Sauce
2 tablespoons olive oil
1 pound ground beef
¼ cup onion, chopped
1 teaspoon chili powder
½ teaspoon ground cumin
½ teaspoon salt
¼ teaspoon pepper
1 (8-ounce) can tomato sauce

Measure flour, cornmeal, buttermilk, baking soda, eggs, and butter into jar of electric blender. Blend for 30 seconds. Scrape down the sides of blender; blend for 1 minute. Refrigerate for 1 hour.

Meanwhile, make sauce. Heat oil in large skillet. Brown meat and onion, stirring frequently. Drain off excess fat. Add chili powder, cumin, salt, pepper, and tomato sauce; simmer for 20 minutes. Keep sauce warm while making crêpes.

Heat lightly oiled skillet or small crêpe pan over moderate heat until a drop of water sizzles and dances on the hot pan; stir batter. Pour a scant 1/4 cup batter into pan and tilt pan in all directions to coat bottom. Cook until bottom is lightly browned and edges appear dry. Turn; cook a few seconds, until lightly browned. Stack on a towel, with paper towels between each. Keep crêpes warm in oven as others are cooked. When all crêpes are made, fill each with some meat mixture; roll crêpes and place on warm platter.

Garnish enchiladas with fresh tomato wedges and parsley. Makes 6 servings.

Beef Enchiladas

2 tablespoons light olive oil
1 cup onion, chopped
2 cloves garlic, finely chopped
1 pound ground beef
2 cups tomato sauce
¾ cup Chili Salsa (see Index)
½ teaspoon salt
1 dozen fresh or frozen tortillas
1½ cups light cream, combined with 1 cup beef broth
½ pound Monterey Jack cheese, grated

In heavy, 2-quart skillet heat oil and cook onion and garlic until onion is translucent. Add ground beef; brown. Add tomato sauce, chili salsa, and salt. Simmer uncovered 10 minutes. Set aside.

Heat 1 inch oil in small, heavy skillet until hot but not smoking. Fry each tortilla a few seconds, but not until crisp. Immediately dip tortilla in cream and broth mixture. Remove and stack.

Boiled Beef

Spread beef mixture on tortillas; roll and place, seam-side-down, in a well-oiled baking pan large enough to hold 12 tortillas. Pour reserved liquid over tortillas. Sprinkle cheese evenly over tortillas and bake in preheated 350°F oven 25 minutes, or until cheese is lightly browned and bubbling hot. Makes 6 servings.

Beef Fillet Mexicana

1 tablespoon butter or margarine	4 servings beef fillet, 4 ounces each (or use rib-eye steaks)
1 large onion, chopped	
1 green pepper, chopped	¼ to ½ teaspoon freshly ground black pepper
1 red pepper, chopped	
2 tablespoons tomato paste	2 tablespoons vegetable oil
½ cup hot beef bouillon	2 tablespoons tequila (or vodka)
¾ teaspoon salt	
⅛ teaspoon white pepper	⅛ teaspoon cayenne pepper
Few drops Tabasco sauce	

Heat butter in frying pan; sauté onion until golden. Add green and red peppers; cook 2 minutes.

Blend tomato paste with hot bouillon; pour over vegetables. Season with 1/2 teaspoon salt, white pepper, and Tabasco. Cover; simmer 10 minutes.

Meanwhile, pat meat dry with paper towels. Rub generously with coarsely ground black pepper. Heat oil in skillet until very hot; cook meat 3 minutes on each side. Arrange vegetables on preheated platter; place steaks on top.

Add tequila or other clear liquor to pan drippings; scrape any particles from bottom of pan. Season with cayenne and 1/4 teaspoon salt. Pour over meat; serve immediately. Makes 4 servings.

Mexican Meat Hash

3 tablespoons oil	½ teaspoon chili powder
½ pound lean ground pork	⅛ teaspoon cumin
½ pound ground beef	Pinch of ground cloves
1 small onion, chopped	½ cup raisins
1 clove garlic, minced	½ teaspoon salt
½ cup tomato catsup	¼ teaspoon ground black pepper
1 teaspoon red wine vinegar	
1 teaspoon ground cinnamon	½ cup toasted, slivered, blanched almonds

Heat oil in large frying pan. Add meats; cook over moderate heat, stirring occasionally, until meat loses its pink color. Add onion and garlic; cook until browned. Add catsup, vinegar, cinnamon, chili powder, cumin, cloves, raisins, salt, and pepper. Stir to blend. Bring mixture to a boil. Reduce heat to simmer; cook for 15 to 20 minutes. Add almonds; stir. Use this mixture to fill tamales, or serve with rice. Makes 4 servings.

American Enchiladas

To make sandwiches with this mixture: Warm flour tortillas in large cast-iron skillet over moderate heat about 30 seconds on each side (just heat them through and make them pliable—do not make them hard and crisp). Fill each with about 1/2 cup meat hash; top each with 3 tablespoons shredded Cheddar cheese and 1/4 cup shredded lettuce. Fold up tortillas like packages by folding bottoms and top edges in 1 inch; then pull the 2 sides to the center, overlapping each other.

Mexican Beef Pie

Pastry for 9-inch, 2-crust pie
2   tablespoons vegetable oil
½   cup onion, chopped
½   cup green pepper, chopped
1   pound ground beef
1   teaspoon salt
¼   teaspoon freshly ground black pepper
1   tablespoon chili powder
1   (8-ounce) can Spanish-style tomato sauce
½   cup sliced stuffed olives

Line 9-inch pie plate with 1/2 the pastry.

Heat oil in skillet; sauté onion and green pepper 5 minutes. Add beef; cook until browned, stirring frequently. Add seasonings and tomato sauce; cook over low heat 15 minutes. Let cool. Add olives. Turn mixture into pastry shell.

Roll out remaining pastry; cut into thin strips. Arrange over meat in lattice pattern. Bake in preheated 400°F oven 35 to 40 minutes, until pastry is well browned. Makes 5 or 6 servings.

Ranch-Style Steaks

Sauce
2   tablespoons olive oil
1   green pepper, cleaned, seeded, and chopped
1   clove garlic, minced
½   cup onion, chopped
2   hot peppers, stemmed, seeded, and chopped
¼   cup tomato catsup
1   cup beef broth
Salt and pepper to taste
½   teaspoon paprika

Steaks
4   fillet steaks (3 ounces each)
4   tablespoons cooking oil
Salt and pepper to taste
Parsley, pickled hot peppers, and tomato wedges

Heat olive oil in small skillet. Add vegetables; sauté for 3 minutes. Add catsup, broth, salt and pepper to taste, and paprika. Reduce heat to low; simmer mixture while cooking steaks.

Slightly flatten steaks. Wipe with a damp cloth; pat dry with a paper towel. Heat cooking oil in heavy skillet over moderately high heat. Sauté steaks for 3 minutes on each side; transfer to a warm platter.

Top steaks with the sauce. Garnish with parsley, tomato wedges, and hot peppers. Makes 4 servings.

Striped Rice with Ground Meat

1⅔ cups rice	Salt
1 bouillon cube	Pepper
1 onion	1 red pepper
Butter	1 green pepper
1 pound ground beef	1 can strained tomatoes
1 can crushed tomatoes	Vegetable broth

Boil rice according to directions on package. Use a bouillon cube instead of salt when preparing rice.

Chop onion and brown it in a little butter. Stir in ground meat with a fork so that it crumbles while browning. Add crushed tomatoes and allow to boil for about 20 minutes. Season with salt and pepper.

Chop each of the peppers separately. Preheat oven to 475°F. Alternate rice and ground meat in an ovenproof dish. Place green and red chopped peppers on top. Dot with a little butter and bake in oven for 15 minutes.

Make sauce using strained tomatoes from a can or fresh tomatoes that are first boiled and then strained. Stir a small amount of vegetable broth into tomatoes, and season with salt and pepper. Makes 4 servings.

Marinated Beef Roast

1 clove garlic, minced	1 (4-pound) rolled rump roast
1 teaspoon ground black pepper	3 tablespoons olive oil
1 bay leaf	2 tablespoons flour
1½ cups dry red wine	2 tablespoons water
2 tablespoons lemon juice	

Combine garlic, pepper, bay leaf, wine, and lemon juice in an enamelware pan or deep glass casserole. Add roast; turn it several times to coat with mixture. Cover; allow to marinate in refrigerator at least 24 hours, turning occasionally.

Heat oil over moderate heat. Remove roast from marinade and pat dry. Brown on all sides in hot oil.

Meanwhile, preheat oven to 375°F. Pour marinade over roast in Dutch oven; cover tightly. Place in oven; cook for 2 hours. Uncover; bake for 30 minutes more. Transfer pan to stove; remove meat to warm platter.

Make a paste with flour and water; thicken the pan gravy. Slice the roast and serve with the gravy and oven-fried potato wedges. Makes 8 to 10 servings.

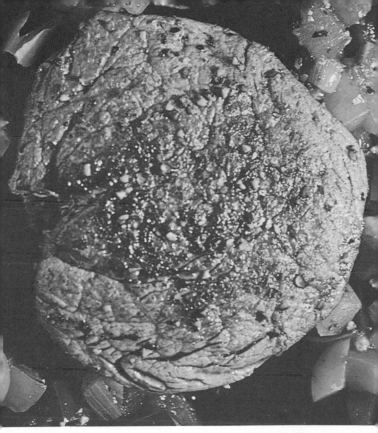

Beef Fillet Mexicana

Tacos

1 **pound ground beef**	**Taco shells**
1½ **teaspoons chili powder**	**Cheddar cheese, shredded**
½ **teaspoon salt**	**Lettuce, shredded**
½ **teaspoon garlic powder**	**Onion, finely chopped**
¼ **teaspoon pepper**	**Tomato, chopped**

Brown ground beef for 5 minutes in skillet. Add spices; stir, then simmer for another 3 minutes.

Spoon 1-1/2 heaping tablespoons of meat mixture into taco shells. Add other ingredients. Top with shredded Cheddar cheese. Makes 10 to 12 tacos.

Beef Stew Mexican-Style

1½ pounds lean stewing beef, cut into cubes	¼ teaspoon pepper
1 large onion, sliced	1 (7-ounce) can green chili salsa
1 clove garlic, minced	
4 tablespoons olive oil	***Beer Rice***
3 tablespoons wine vinegar	2 tablespoons olive oil
½ cup tomato sauce	1 cup raw long-grain rice
1 cup red wine	1 (10¾-ounce) can condensed onion soup
1 bay leaf	
1 teaspoon oregano	1 (10¾-ounce) soup can of beer
½ teaspoon salt	

Combine all ingredients in large saucepan. Bring mixture to a boil, stirring occasionally. Reduce heat to simmer; cook for 3 hours or until meat falls apart.

Make beer rice: Heat olive oil in medium saucepan over moderate heat. Add rice; brown lightly, stirring constantly. Add onion soup and beer. Cover tightly; simmer for 20 to 25 minutes or until all liquid is absorbed.

Serve stew with the beer rice. Makes 4 servings.

Swiss Steak Mexican-Style

3 tablespoons flour	1½ cups fresh mushrooms, sliced
½ teaspoon seasoned salt	
⅛ teaspoon pepper	2 cups canned tomatoes
1½ pounds bottom round steak	1½ teaspoons chili powder
3 tablespoons oil	1 teaspoon sugar
1 large onion, sliced	¼ cup red wine
1 clove garlic, minced	1 tablespoon water
	Salt and pepper to taste

Combine 2 tablespoons of flour, seasoned salt, and pepper. Dredge steak in flour mixture. Heat oil in electric skillet or large, heavy skillet. Brown steaks well on both sides. Remove from pan. Add onion, garlic, and mushrooms; sauté for 5 minutes, stirring occasionally.

Puree tomatoes in electric blender with chili powder, sugar, and wine. Add to vegetables in skillet.

Return meat to skillet. Coat with sauce. Bring to a boil, reduce heat to low, and cover. Simmer for 2 to 2-1/2 hours or until tender. Combine flour and water to form a paste. Remove steaks from skillet; keep them warm. Slowly add flour and water paste to gravy, stirring well. Cook over low heat until thickened. Serve the steaks and gravy with hot cooked rice. Makes 4 servings.

Mexican Beef Pie

Tamale Pie

½ pound ground beef
½ pound bulk pork sausage
1 large onion, sliced
⅛ teaspoon garlic, minced
1 (16-ounce) can tomatoes with juice
1 (12-ounce) can whole-kernel corn, drained
1 tablespoon chili powder
1 teaspoon salt
¼ teaspoon pepper

Cornmeal Pastry
1 cup cornmeal
2 medium eggs
1 cup milk
18 green olives, chopped

Olive slices for garnish

Cook meats with onion and garlic until browned. Stir in tomatoes with juice, corn, and seasonings. Simmer for 10 minutes. Pour into greased oblong baking dish.

Prepare cornmeal crust by mixing cornmeal, eggs, milk, and chopped olives. Spread over hot mixture. Decorate top with a few olive slices. Bake at 350°F for 30 to 35 minutes. Serve tamale pie warm. Makes 4 to 6 servings.

Beef Tacos with Mexican Sauce

Mexican Sauce
2 cups peeled tomatoes, chopped, or 1 (16-ounce) can whole tomatoes and juice
1 small onion, chopped
1 clove garlic, chopped
1 tablespoon chili powder
½ teaspoon oregano
1 teaspoon salt
Few drops of hot sauce

Taco Shells
12 to 18 fresh or frozen (thawed) tortillas

Taco Filling
2 pounds lean ground beef
2 medium onions, finely chopped

1 or 2 tablespoons chili powder
1 teaspoon oregano
1 teaspoon paprika
2 teaspoons salt
1 tablespoon Worcestershire sauce
⅓ cup Mexican sauce

Taco Garnishes
Shredded lettuce
Shredded cheese
Chopped tomatoes
Chopped onions
Mexican sauce

Combine all sauce ingredients in a food processor or blender container; blend until smooth. Pour into small saucepan; simmer for 30 minutes. Use on top of taco filling. Makes 2-1/2 to 3 cups.

To make folded, crisp-fried tacos, fry 1 corn or flour tortilla at a time in about 1/2 inch hot oil over medium heat, until it becomes soft (just a few seconds). With tongs or 2 forks, fold it in half and hold slightly, so there is a space between halves for the filling to be added later.

Fry each tortilla until crisp and light brown, turning it in oil to cook all sides. The entire cooking procedure takes only minutes for each shell. To keep fried shells warm until ready to fill, place them on a paper-towel-lined baking sheet in a 200°F oven as long as 10 or 15 minutes.

To make taco filling, brown meat and onions; drain well. Add chili powder, oregano, paprika, salt, Worcestershire sauce, and Mexican sauce. Serve hot. Season more to taste. This freezes well.

To assemble tacos, place desired amount of meat filling in center of each fried taco shell; top filling with garnishes such as shredded lettuce, shredded cheese, and Mexican sauce. Serve tacos hot. Makes 12 to 18 tacos.

Leg of Lamb Mexican-Style

2 cloves garlic	Salt and pepper
1 tablespoon dried oregano	2 tablespoons wine vinegar
⅛ teaspoon ground cumin	3 tablespoons olive oil
2 teaspoons chili powder	1 onion, chopped
1 (4- to 5-pound) leg of lamb	

Peel garlic; mash with oregano and cumin. Add a few drops of water, so that mixture forms a stiff paste. Stir in chili powder.

Wipe leg of lamb with damp cloth. With sharp knife make incisions all over surface of lamb. Put some spice mixture in each incision. Rub roast with salt and pepper.

Combine vinegar, olive oil, and onion. Put roast in large plastic bag; pour oil and vinegar mixture over roast. Tie bag shut; marinate roast overnight.

Bring roast to room temperature. Roast lamb in open pan at 325°F for 30 minutes per pound. Serve lamb with pan-roasted potatoes. Makes 8 to 10 servings.

Mexican Lamb

4 cups milk	4 cups cooked rice
1 onion, chopped	½ cup raisins (cook with the rice)
2 bay leaves	
½ teaspoon dried thyme	½ cup sliced canned peaches
1 teaspoon salt	½ cup sliced canned pears
¼ teaspoon pepper	½ cup sliced almonds, toasted
¼ cup butter	
2 pounds lamb, trimmed well and cut into cubes	2 tablespoons fresh parsley

Combine milk, onion, bay leaves, thyme, salt, and pepper. Heat mixture, but do not boil. Heat butter in a skillet; sauté lamb until golden. Add lamb to hot milk. Simmer uncovered over low heat until lamb is tender and milk has cooked away (about 1 hour or more).

Place lamb in center of serving dish that has been covered with the hot rice and raisin mixture. Arrange sliced peaches and pears around lamb. Sprinkle lamb with almonds and parsley. Makes 4 to 6 servings.

Striped Rice with Ground Meat

Tamales

24 corn husks (dried) or 24 (6-inch) squares of cooking parchment	**Tamale Filling** 1½ cups Pork in Red Chili Sauce (see Index) or Mexican Meat Hash (see Index) or 1½ cups cooked shredded meat mixed with Red Chili Sauce (see Index) to moisten or 24 small cheese slices (1 × 3 inches)
Tamale Dough 1 cup lard 2½ cups instant Masa Harina ½ teaspoon salt 1¾ cups chicken broth	24 small strips of green chili

Soak corn husks in hot water to cover, if used.

Next make the dough. Beat lard with electric mixer until light. Add masa, salt, and chicken broth; beat until light and fluffy. Divide into 24 equal parts.

Drain corn husks; pat dry. Place each portion masa dough on parchment square or corn husk; spread to form a 4-inch square, keeping 1 side even with 1 edge of the paper or husk. Top with 1 tablespoon of filling, or 1 slice of cheese plus 1 strip of chili pepper. Roll up as for a jelly roll, starting with the side of the dough that is even with the side of the paper or husk. Fold the ends over, sealing well.

The tamales are cooked by steaming. A steamer pot is ideal (the kind used for crabs or corn), but one can be easily improvised. Select a large, deep pot. Place a vegetable steaming basket or metal colander in bottom of pan. Line steamer or colander with any leftover corn husks. Bring 1 to 2 inches of water to boil in bottom of kettle or steamer pot.

Meanwhile, place tamales upright in steamer, packing tightly. Place basket in steamer kettle; cover tightly. Steam for 1 hour or until dough no longer sticks to paper. Serve tamales hot with chili sauce (for example: Red Chili Sauce). Makes 24 tamales.

Pork Kebabs Yucatan

Juice of 1 lime ¼ cup salad oil ¼ teaspoon crushed whole coriander ¼ cup onion, chopped 1 clove garlic, mashed ¼ teaspoon pepper	1¼ pounds lean pork, cut in 1½-inch cubes 1 medium zucchini, sliced 2 red peppers, stemmed, seeded, and cut in chunks ½ pound mushrooms, cleaned and stems cut off

Beef Stew Mexican Style

The day before cooking, combine lime juice, oil, coriander, onion, garlic, and pepper in a glass or pottery bowl or casserole. Add meat; stir to coat with marinade. Cover; refrigerate 24 hours, stirring once or twice.

To cook, drain meat, reserving marinade. Skewer meat alternately with zucchini, red peppers, and mushrooms. Broil until done through (20 to 25 minutes), basting occasionally with marinade. Serve kebabs with cooked rice. Makes 4 servings.

Pork Rolls

1 **pound lean pork, ground once**	1 **tablespoon parsley**
¼ **teaspoon pepper**	1 **cup soft bread crumbs (about)**
1½ **teaspoons garlic powder**	1 **cup flour**
1 **teaspoon salt**	**Olive oil**
1 **egg, beaten**	

Mix pork, pepper, garlic powder, salt, egg, and parsley together. Add enough bread crumbs to bind mixture together. Form mixture into 6 small rolls. Dredge rolls in flour. Fry in hot olive oil until golden brown and thoroughly cooked; drain. Makes 6 servings.

Pork Roast Cooked in Beer with Green Sauce

2 **medium onions, chopped**	*Green Sauce*
2 **carrots, peeled and sliced**	2 **tablespoons olive oil**
1 **(4- to 5-pound) loin or shoulder pork roast**	1 **medium onion, chopped**
2 **teaspoons salt**	1 **clove garlic, peeled and chopped**
½ **teaspoon oregano**	1 **(10-ounce) can Mexican green tomatoes (tomatillos)**
½ **teaspoon ground coriander**	½ **teaspoon crumbled dried oregano**
½ to ¾ **cup beer**	½ **teaspoon dried cilantro**
	2 **tablespoons wine vinegar**
	Salt and pepper

Place onions and carrots in roasting pan. Rub pork with salt, oregano, and coriander. Place pork on top of vegetables; add beer. Cover; roast at 350°F for 2-3/4 hours. Add more beer, if necessary.

To make green sauce, heat olive oil in small skillet. Sauté onion and garlic until limp. Drain tomatillos; reserve liquid. In electric blender or food processor, combine tomatillos, 1/2 cup reserved liquid, onion, garlic, and olive oil, oregano, and cilantro; puree.

Heat skillet once again over moderate heat. Pour in sauce; cook for 10 minutes. Remove from heat; add wine vinegar and salt and pepper to taste. Chill sauce and serve with pork roast. Makes 6 to 8 servings.

Pork Fillets

2	pounds pork tenderloin	1	teaspoon salt
1	large apple	¼	teaspoon freshly ground
2	tablespoons almonds,		pepper
	chopped	¼	cup olive oil
1	teaspoon sugar	½	cup dry red wine
¼	teaspoon cinnamon	1	cup stock
¼	teaspoon garlic powder		

Slice tenderloin into 6 pieces. Peel, core, and finely chop apple. Combine apple, almonds, sugar, and cinnamon; mix well. Make slash in center of each tenderloin. Stuff with apple filling. Press meat together; secure with metal clamps if necessary.

Combine garlic powder, salt, and pepper. Rub tenderloins with mixture. Heat oil in deep skillet. Brown tenderloins on all sides. Add wine and stock; bring to boil. Reduce heat; simmer 1 hour, turning meat at 15-minute intervals. Makes 4 servings.

Pork Spareribs in Mexican Barbecue Sauce

Mexican Barbecue Sauce		2	large tomatoes, peeled and
1	tablespoon olive oil		cut up
1	medium onion, chopped	2	tablespoons chili powder
1	clove garlic, peeled and	2	tablespoons sugar
	minced	¼	cup vinegar
1	fresh chili pepper,	⅓	cup olive oil
	stemmed, seeded, and	¼	cup beer
	chopped		
½	tablespoon salt	4	pounds pork spareribs
			(country-style)

First make the sauce. Heat the tablespoon of olive oil in saucepan. Sauté onion in oil until lightly browned. Add garlic, chopped chili, salt, and tomatoes; simmer until mixture thickens. Add remaining sauce ingredients; cook for 8 minutes, stirring constantly. Marinate spareribs in sauce for several hours before grilling (if possible).

Grill over hot charcoal, basting periodically with sauce, until tender, well browned, and crusty. Pour extra sauce on the ribs before serving. Makes 6 to 8 servings.

Pork Kebabs Yucatan

Mexican Sausage (Chorizo)

1	pound lean pork shoulder	½	teaspoon freshly ground
2	tablespoons vinegar		black pepper
1	teaspoon crushed oregano	1	teaspoon salt
1	clove garlic, mashed	⅛	teaspoon ground cumin
2	tablespoons chili powder		

Coarsely grind pork shoulder. Add vinegar, oregano, garlic, chili powder, pepper, salt, and cumin. Mix thoroughly with your hands. Pack into crock or glass jar; store in refrigerator up to 2 weeks, or freeze. Makes 1 pound of sausage meat or the equivalent of 5 purchased chorizo links.

Note: Use 1/3 cup of the mixture for each commercial sausage link called for in a recipe.

Chick-Peas with Garlic Sausage

2 cups dried chick-peas	2 cloves garlic, minced
1 pound chorizos or other garlic-flavored sausage	1 large green pepper, seeded and sliced into strips
2 tablespoons olive oil	1½ cups tomato sauce
1 large Spanish onion, chopped	1 teaspoon salt

Wash chick-peas; place in large Dutch oven. Cover with cold water; soak overnight. Next day bring chick-peas to boil. Reduce heat to simmer; cook 2 hours or until tender, but still retain their shape.

Prick sausage with fork. Place in shallow skillet; cover with cold water. Bring water to boil. Boil sausage 5 minutes; drain. Slice into 1/4-inch slices.

Heat oil. Fry sausage until brown. Remove from oil. Add onion and garlic; sauté 8 minutes. Add pepper; sauté until peppers are limp but still crisp. Add chick-peas, sausage, tomato sauce, and salt to skillet; stir. Simmer 15 minutes or until thoroughly heated. Makes 8 servings.

Veal with Mexican Sauce

Mexican Sauce	4 veal steaks, cubed
2 cups tomatoes, chopped and peeled, or 1 (16-ounce) can whole tomatoes and juice	2 eggs, beaten
	1 cup dry bread crumbs
	Salt and pepper
1 small onion, chopped	½ cup butter
1 clove garlic, chopped	½ cup Monterey Jack cheese, shredded
1 green pepper, chopped	
1 tablespoon chili powder	
½ teaspoon oregano	
1 teaspoon salt	
Few drops of hot sauce	

Combine all sauce ingredients in food processor or blender container; blend until smooth. Pour into small saucepan; simmer for 30 minutes. Makes 2-1/2 to 3 cups sauce.

Dip veal in beaten eggs. Coat with bread crumbs, salt, and pepper. Fry in butter until browned; drain. Put veal in pan, cover with sauce, and top with shredded cheese. Bake at 350°F for 20 minutes. Makes 4 servings.

Chicken Bread Pies

3 tablespoons olive oil	½ teaspoon garlic powder
½ cup onion, chopped	½ teaspoon salt
½ cup green pepper, chopped	Dash of cayenne
½ cup Serrano ham, chopped	1 box hot-roll mix
1½ cups tomatoes, peeled and chopped	1 cup warm water
½ cup chick-peas	1 egg, beaten
	1 egg white, unbeaten

Heat oil in a skillet. Add onion and green pepper; sauté until tender. Add ham, tomatoes, chick-peas, garlic powder, salt, and cayenne. Simmer until mixture thickens and holds its shape in spoon.

Dissolve yeast from hot-roll mix in warm water as directed on package. Add beaten egg; blend well. Add flour mixture to yeast mixture; blend well. Cover; let rise in warm place until double in bulk.

Punch down dough; place on well-floured surface. Roll out to 16 × 20-inch rectangle. Cut into 4-inch squares. Fill each square with heaping tablespoon of chicken mixture. Bring corners together; pinch edges together. Place on greased cookie sheet, pinched-edges-down. Let rise 30 minutes. Brush with egg white. Bake at 350°F 30 minutes. Makes 6 servings.

Company Chicken and Rice Casserole

3 tablespoons olive oil	2 cups cooked chicken, boned, skinned, and shredded
½ cup onion, chopped	
1 cup raw long-grain rice	¾ cup sour cream
2 cups chicken broth	½ cup stuffed green olives, sliced
3 tablespoons dry sherry	
1 bay leaf	
Salt and pepper	
1 teaspoon dried cilantro (dried coriander leaves)	

Heat oil in large, heavy skillet. Sauté onion until limp. Add rice; cook, stirring occasionally, until lightly browned. Add chicken broth, sherry, bay leaf, salt and pepper to taste, cilantro, and chicken. Stir well.

Bring mixture to a boil. Cover, reduce heat to simmer, and cook for 20 minutes or until all liquid is absorbed. Uncover; stir in sour cream. Over very low heat, cook just long enough to heat through. Top chicken with sliced olives, and serve. Makes 4 servings.

Pork Fillets

Chicken Cooked in Foil

1	(2½- to 3-pound) chicken	½	cup green chilies, chopped
2	tablespoons olive oil	2	tablespoons fresh cilantro
Salt and pepper			(or 2 teaspoons dried
1	medium onion, finely		cilantro), chopped
	chopped	2	fresh tomatoes, peeled and
1	clove garlic, minced		chopped

Wash chicken, drain, and pat dry. Cut chicken into quarters. Cut 4, 10-inch squares of heavy-duty foil. Divide oil among the 4 sheets of foil. Grease foil. Place a chicken piece on each foil sheet; grease. Salt and pepper chicken to taste.

Combine onion, garlic, chilies, cilantro, and tomatoes in small bowl. Spoon some sauce over each piece of chicken; fold foil into a neat, sealed package. Place on cookie sheet; bake at 425°F for 40 minutes. Carefully open foil packages and allow steam to escape.

Serve from foil packages with a crisp green salad. Makes 4 servings.

Chicken Cooked in Foil

Chicken Cooked with Corn

1 (2½- to 3-pound) broiler-fryer chicken
4 tablespoons butter or margarine
Salt and pepper
1 (16½-ounce) can whole-kernel corn, drained, and the liquid reserved
½ cup green chilies, chopped (optional)

Sauce
3 tablespoons butter or margarine
2 tablespoons flour
1 cup half and half
2 eggs, separated
Salt and white pepper
¼ teaspoon nutmeg
2 tablespoons bread crumbs
2 tablespoons butter

Wash chicken, pat dry, and cut into quarters. Heat butter or margarine in heavy skillet. Brown chicken on all sides. Place in an ovenproof casserole. Season chicken with salt and pepper to taste. Add corn and chilies (if used) to juices in skillet along with 1/4 cup reserved corn liquid. Stir well; pour over chicken.

Next make the sauce. Melt butter or margarine in saucepan. Add flour; cook until evenly and lightly browned, stirring constantly. Add half and half all at once; cook over medium heat, stirring, until slightly thickened. Beat egg yolks, salt, pepper, and nutmeg together. Add some hot sauce to egg yolks; beat well. Pour egg-yolk mixture into saucepan; mix well. Remove from the heat.

Beat egg whites until stiff but not dry; fold into sauce. Pour sauce over chicken, sprinkle with bread crumbs, and dot with butter. Bake in a preheated 350°F oven for 45 minutes. Makes 4 servings.

Chicken Pepper Stew

1	(3-pound) broiler-fryer	2	large onions, chopped
5	large carrots	2	cups cabbage, shredded
1	tablespoon salt	1	(6-ounce) can tomato
5	white peppercorns		puree (optional)
5	whole allspice	½	teaspoon chili pepper,
1	bay leaf		minced
3	whole cloves	1	cup ground peanuts
1	leek, chopped	1	cup boiled rice

Place chicken in a large saucepan; add enough water to cover. Bring to a boil; skim well.

Dice 1 carrot, add to chicken with salt, peppercorns, allspice, bay leaf, cloves, and leek. Cook about 40 minutes or until chicken is tender. Remove chicken from broth; cool. Strain broth; add enough water, if needed, to make 4 cups liquid. Reserve 1/2 cup broth for later use; pour remaining broth back into saucepan.

Grate remaining carrots; add to broth with onions, cabbage, tomato puree, and chili pepper. Bring to a boil; reduce heat. Cook, stirring frequently, until thickened and vegetables are tender. Add peanuts; cook 15 minutes longer, stirring frequently.

Remove skin and bones from chicken; cut chicken into large pieces. Combine reserved broth with chicken in heavy saucepan; heat through. Place chicken, vegetable mixture, and rice in separate serving dishes. Place rice, then chicken, then vegetable mixture in soup bowls to serve. Makes 6 servings.

Sour-Cream Chicken Enchiladas

Enchilada Sauce

1	clove garlic, minced
2	small onions, chopped
3	tablespoons oil
2	tablespoons flour
1¾ cups chicken bouillon	
2	(5-ounce) cans green chilies, drained and chopped
2	cups canned tomatoes, drained well and chopped (2, 28-ounce cans)

Enchiladas

12	corn tortillas, fresh or frozen (thawed)
1	pint sour cream
½	pound New York white Cheddar, shredded
4	cups cooked chicken, shredded
Extra cheese (shredded) and black olive slices for topping (if desired)	

To make sauce, sauté garlic and onions in oil. Add flour; stir in bouillon. Cook, stirring constantly, about 5 minutes, until thickened. Add chilies and tomatoes; allow to simmer for 5 to 10 minutes. Makes 3-1/2 to 4 cups of sauce.

To assemble enchiladas, dip tortillas in hot oil to soften. Drain well on paper towels. Mix sour cream, shredded cheese, and chicken. Place filling in center of each tortilla; roll them up. Use approximately 1/2 cup filling per tortilla. Place rolled enchiladas side-by-side in a large baking dish; pour sauce over them. Sprinkle with extra cheese and sliced black olives if desired. Bake at 350°F for about 30 minutes, until bubbly and hot. Makes 6 servings (2 enchiladas each).

Chicken, Seafood, and Rice

1	(2½- to 3-pound) broiler-fryer chicken, cut up
¼	cup olive oil
1	cup water
3	tablespoons olive oil
1	medium onion, chopped
1	clove garlic, minced
1½ cups raw long-grain white rice	
2	teaspoons chicken-broth granules
¼	cup white wine

⅛	teaspoon saffron
⅛	teaspoon cayenne
1	teaspoon salt
Boiling water	
2	tomatoes, peeled and cut in quarters
½	cup ham, finely chopped
2	cups fresh or frozen raw shrimp, peeled and deveined
1	(10-ounce) package frozen peas, thawed

Wash chicken and pat dry. Heat 1/4 cup oil in skillet; sauté chicken until well browned on all sides. Add water. Reduce heat to low; cook 20 minutes. Cool chicken; reserve pan juices.

Chicken-Pepper Stew

Heat 3 tablespoons oil in Dutch oven. Sauté onion and garlic until limp. Add rice; sauté until lightly browned.

In large measuring cup, combine chicken-broth granules, wine, saffron, cayenne pepper, and salt; add enough boiling water to make 3 cups liquid. Add liquid to Dutch oven along with chicken, tomatoes, ham, and shrimp. Stir well. Cover; bring just to a boil. Reduce heat to low; cook for 20 minutes. Add peas; cook 10 minutes more. Makes 5 to 6 servings.

Chicken and Taco Chips Casserole

9 taco shells or 1 (12-ounce) bag taco chips	2 cups sharp Cheddar cheese, grated
2 whole chicken breasts, cooked and chopped	1 (10-ounce) can tomatoes and green chilies
1 (10½-ounce) can chicken and rice soup	

Crush taco chips in a bowl. Place a layer of crushed chips in bottom of greased 1-quart casserole. Sprinkle a layer of chopped chicken over chips. Pour several spoonfuls of condensed chicken and rice soup over the chicken layer. Sprinkle with a layer of grated cheese.

Pour several spoonfuls of tomato and green chili mixture over cheese layer. Repeat process of layering chips, chicken, soup, cheese, and chilies until all ingredients are used. Top casserole with additional grated cheese if desired. Bake for 25 minutes at 350°F.

This may be prepared ahead and refrigerated before baking. It freezes well before and after baking. Makes 4 to 6 servings.

Tablecloth Stainer

2 tablespoons butter or margarine	2 cups chicken stock
2 tablespoons cooking oil	½ cup white wine
1 pound boneless pork, cut into 1-inch chunks	¼ cup sugar
1 (4- to 5-pound) roasting chicken, disjointed	1½ teaspoons cinnamon
½ cup flour	1 tablespoon chili powder
	3 cloves
Sauce	1 bay leaf
1 tablespoon blanched, slivered almonds	1 sweet potato, peeled and cut into cubes
2 teaspoons sesame seeds	1 medium apple
1 medium onion, chopped	1 cup pineapple chunks, drained
1 green pepper, seeded, and chopped	2 medium bananas (optional)
1 (16-ounce) can tomatoes, broken up with a fork	

Heat butter and oil together in Dutch oven. Sauté pork until well browned. Dredge chicken in flour; brown well. Reserve meats while making sauce.

Add 1 tablespoon of oil to pan, if necessary. Sauté almonds, sesame seeds, onion, and pepper until lightly browned. Add tomatoes; simmer for 10 minutes. Puree sauce in blender.

In Dutch oven, combine pureed sauce, chicken stock, wine, sugar, cinnamon, chili powder, cloves, and bay leaf. Add chicken and pork. Bring to a boil. Reduce heat to low; cook for 30 minutes. Add sweet potato; cook 15 minutes more.

Peel, core, and dice apple. Add apple and pineapple to stew; heat through. Serve stew in bowls. Peel and slice bananas into individual bowls as the stew is served. Makes 6 servings.

Steamed Fish in Tomato Sauce

Tostadas

Sauce
- ½ cup onion
- 2 tablespoons olive oil
- 1½ cups canned tomatoes, drained and cut up
- 3 tablespoons canned green chilies, chopped
- 2 tablespoons cilantro, chopped
- (2 4-ounce cans taco sauce may be substituted for the sauce)

Tostadas
- Vegetable oil for frying
- 8 corn tortillas (6 to 7 inches in diameter)
- 2 cups Refried Beans (see Index)
- 1½ cups Monterey Jack cheese, grated
- 3 cups cooked chicken breast, cubed
- 3 cups iceberg lettuce, shredded
- 1 large ripe avocado
- 2 tablespoons lemon juice

First make sauce. Sauté onion in hot oil until lightly browned. Add tomatoes and chilies; cook over low heat until thick. Add cilantro; cool.

To assemble tostadas, heat oil over moderate heat in heavy 8-inch frying pan until quite hot. Fry tortillas, 1 at a time, flat, until crisp; drain on paper towels. Spread tortillas with beans; sprinkle with cheese, chicken, and lettuce. Peel and slice avocado; dip avocado slices in lemon juice and place on top of tostadas. Top with sauce. Serve. Makes 4 servings.

Variation: Spread tortillas with beans and serve rest of ingredients in small bowls on the table so that each person can assemble his own tostada.

Fiesta Turkey in Mole Sauce

- 1 (10- to 12-pound) turkey, disjointed
- ¼ cup cooking oil
- 1 teaspoon salt
- Water

Mole Sauce
- 6 dried Ancho chilies
- Boiling water
- 2 tablespoons oil
- 1 medium onion, chopped
- 2 cloves garlic, minced
- ½ teaspoon chilies, crushed
- 1 cup canned Italian plum tomatoes, chopped
- ¾ teaspoon ground cinnamon
- ½ teaspoon ground cloves
- ¼ teaspoon ground coriander
- ¼ teaspoon anise
- ¼ teaspoon cumin
- 1 dry tortilla, cut into pieces
- ¼ cup sesame seeds
- ¼ cup raisins
- 2 cups chicken broth
- 2 (1-ounce) squares semisweet chocolate, grated

Wash turkey; pat dry. Heat oil in Dutch oven; brown turkey well on all sides, adding more oil if necessary to keep turkey from sticking. Add salt and enough water to cover. Bring to a boil. Cover; reduce heat to low. Cook 1 hour or until tender. Set aside.

Meanwhile, prepare sauce. Stem and seed red chilies under cold running water. Tear chilies into pieces; soak in boiling water to cover for 30 minutes. Drain; reserve 1/4 cup soaking liquid.

Heat oil in skillet. Sauté onion and garlic until limp. In blender jar combine Ancho chilies, reserved liquid, onion, garlic, crushed chilies, tomatoes, and spices; puree until smooth. Add tortilla, sesame seeds, and raisins; puree, scraping blender container frequently.

Heat skillet in which onion was cooked over moderate heat for several minutes. Pour puree into skillet; add chicken broth, stirring well. Simmer for 10 minutes. Remove from heat and add chocolate. Stir until chocolate melts. Drain broth from turkey. Pour sauce over turkey; heat through. Serve turkey garnished with sesame seeds. Makes 8 to 10 servings.

Note: The turkey could be roasted unstuffed, sliced, and served with mole sauce if you prefer. Mole sauce is a long and complicated business. It is available in Latin American grocery stores and specialty stores canned and as a powder. It is reconstituted with broth before serving. Chicken and pork are also served with this sauce.

Poached Fish with Avocado Sauce

1½ to 2 pounds frozen fish fillets, thawed	1 lemon (cut in half— squeeze 1 half, slice other half)
2 onions, thinly sliced	
2 lemons, thinly sliced	
2 tablespoons butter, melted	*Avocado Sauce*
2 teaspoons salt	2 mashed avocados
1 bay leaf	½ cup sour cream
½ teaspoon black pepper	2 tablespoons lemon juice
3 cups water	½ small onion, finely chopped

Cut fillets into serving portions. Combine onions and lemon slices with butter, salt, bay leaf, and black pepper in an ovenproof baking dish. Place fillets on top of onion and lemon slices; add water. Cover; cook at 350°F for 45 minutes.

Before serving, carefully remove fish fillets with slotted spoon or spatula. Place on heated platter. Sprinkle with juice from 1/2 lemon. Garnish with additional lemon slices.

Prepare Avocado Sauce by mixing all sauce ingredients well. Serve the hot fish with the sauce, or chill the fish and serve it cold. Makes 6 servings.

Fried Fish with Mexican Sauce

1 **pound firm fish fillets, defrosted if frozen (flounder or sole)**	1 **clove garlic, minced**
2 **tablespoons lemon juice**	1 **cup canned peeled tomatoes, drained and chopped**
½ **teaspoon salt**	2 **tablespoons dry sherry**
¼ **teaspoon pepper**	**Salt and pepper**
½ **cup flour**	1 **large pinch saffron**
¼ **cup cooking oil**	

Mexican Sauce

2 **tablespoons olive oil**
1 **small onion, chopped**
½ **cup green pepper, chopped**
¼ **cup celery, chopped**

2 **tablespoons parsley, chopped (for garnish)**

Sprinkle fish fillets with lemon juice, salt, and pepper; set aside while making sauce.

Heat olive oil in saucepan or small skillet. Add onion, green pepper, celery, and garlic; sauté until limp. Add tomatoes, sherry, salt and pepper to taste, and saffron. Stir well; simmer while frying fish.

Drain fish well. Heat cooking oil over moderate heat in large frying pan. Dip fish in flour, coating well; fry until golden, turning once. Drain fish and serve hot, topped with the sauce. Garnish with chopped parsley. Makes 4 servings.

Steamed Fish in Tomato Sauce

2 **pounds whitefish fillets**	6 **medium tomatoes, peeled, seeded, and chopped**
1 **small onion, peeled and quartered**	1 **teaspoon paprika**
1 **bay leaf**	**Dash of cayenne**
2 **tablespoons olive oil**	1 **teaspoon chives, chopped**
1 **garlic clove, minced**	⅓ **cup white wine**
½ **cup onion, chopped**	**Vinegar**

Place fish, quartered onion, and bay leaf on large piece of aluminum foil. Securely close foil. Place fish in steamer; steam 25 minutes or until fish flakes easily.

Heat oil in deep skillet. Add garlic and chopped onion; sauté until tender. Add tomatoes, paprika, cayenne, chives, and wine. Simmer 30 minutes. Place fish on serving platter; top with tomato sauce. Serve with vinegar. Makes 4 to 6 servings.

Boiled Shrimp with Sauces

Steamed White Asparagus with Garlic Mayonnaise

Spanish-Style Swordfish

1	pound swordfish, cut in very thin slices	1	tablespoon parsley, minced
¼	cup olive oil	1	clove garlic, crushed
2	tablespoons Amontillado sherry	½	teaspoon salt
		¼	cup onion, finely chopped

Arrange swordfish in large shallow pan, cover with remaining ingredients, and marinate at least 1 hour. Remove from marinade; broil 4 inches from heat until lightly browned on each side, using reduced flame.

Serve marinade as sauce, passed separately. Makes 3 to 4 servings.

Fried Fish with Sour Sauce

1 **pound firm white fish, cut into steaks or fillets**	1 **egg, well beaten**
¾ **teaspoon salt**	2 **tablespoons water**
1 **large onion, sliced**	¾ **cup cornmeal**
½ **cup olive oil**	½ **cup red wine vinegar**
1 **clove garlic, minced**	3 **tablespoons olive oil**
½ **cup water**	¼ **cup sliced Spanish olives**
1 **bay leaf**	**stuffed with pimientos**
6 **whole peppercorns**	¼ **cup onion, chopped**
½ **teaspoon coriander seeds, toasted**	

Sprinkle fish with salt; let stand 1/2 hour.

Meanwhile, slowly fry onion in 1/2 cup olive oil in heavy frying pan. Do not brown. Add garlic; continue to fry for a few minutes. Remove onion and garlic from oil with a slotted spoon; place in a small saucepan. Add 1/2 cup water, bay leaf, peppercorns, and coriander; simmer while frying fish.

Beat egg and 2 tablespoons water together. Dip fish in egg wash, then in cornmeal, coating well. Fry in seasoned olive oil until well browned. Drain on paper towels; place on warm platter.

Add vinegar and 3 tablespoons olive oil to onion and spice mixture. Remove bay leaf, peppercorns, and coriander seeds. Pour sauce over fish and garnish with sliced olives and chopped onion. Makes 4 servings.

Red Snapper Veracruz

1 to 1¼ **pounds red-snapper fillets (4 fillets)**	½ **cup onion, chopped**
2 **tablespoons lemon juice**	1 **clove garlic, minced**
Salt and pepper	2 **cups canned tomatoes, chopped**
2 **tablespoons capers, chopped**	¼ **teaspoon crumbled thyme**
¼ **cup sliced pimiento-stuffed green olives**	¼ **teaspoon crumbled marjoram**
2 **tablespoons olive oil**	½ **teaspoon crumbled oregano**

Lightly oil small ovenproof baking dish, big enough to hold fish fillets in a single layer. Arrange fish in baking dish. Sprinkle with lemon juice; salt and pepper lightly. Sprinkle with capers and sliced olives.

Heat oil in small skillet. Add onion and garlic; cook until limp. Add tomatoes, thyme, marjoram, and oregano; simmer for 10 minutes. Pour over fish. Cover baking dish; bake at 350°F for 25 to 30 minutes or until fish flakes easily with a fork.

Serve fish with small, boiled new potatoes. Makes 4 servings.

Fish Yucatan-Style

1 whole fish, such as pompano or snapper	1 teaspoon annatto (achiote)
Juice of 1 lemon	2 tablespoons fresh cilantro, chopped, or 2 tablespoons chopped parsley
Salt and pepper to taste	
4 tablespoons olive oil	Juice of 1 orange
1 onion, finely chopped	2 hard-cooked eggs, chopped
3 ounces green olives, chopped	
1 (1-ounce) can pimiento, chopped, with liquid	

Marinate fish for 15 minutes in lemon juice, salt, and pepper. Heat olive oil in a skillet and sauté onion until limp. Add olives, pimiento and liquid, annatto, cilantro, salt, and pepper. Cook for a few minutes and add orange juice.

Put fish in buttered casserole, cover with sauce, and cook in a 400°F oven for 1/2 hour or until tender. Garnish with chopped eggs. Makes 6 servings.

Grilled Shrimp with Barbecue Sauce

Barbecue Sauce

2 cups catsup	1½ tablespoons liquid smoke
1 cup water	1 teaspoon salt
½ cup cider vinegar	½ teaspoon basil
¾ cup sugar	½ teaspoon oregano
½ cup onion, chopped	½ teaspoon cinnamon
½ cup green pepper, chopped	2 tablespoons butter
½ cup celery, chopped	1 pound medium shrimp (30 to 32 count)
¼ cup parsley, chopped	¼ cup dry sherry or white wine
2 cloves garlic, minced	Heavy foil
1 lemon, whole	
⅛ teaspoon hot-pepper sauce	
1½ tablespoons Worcestershire sauce	

In a pan, combined catsup, water, vinegar, sugar, onion, pepper, celery, parsley, and garlic. Squeeze juice from lemon, cut off ends, and discard seeds; add rinds and juice to sauce. Add hot-pepper sauce, Worcestershire sauce, liquid smoke, salt, basil, oregano, cinnamon, and butter. Cook, uncovered, over medium heat, stirring often, until reduced to 1 quart—approximately 35 minutes. Cool, cover, and chill for storage up to 1 week. Makes 1 quart.

Corn Casserole with Ham and Cheese

Clean 1 pound shrimp without removing shells. Wrap shrimp in heavy foil, pouring in 1-1/2 cups barbecue sauce before sealing packet. Refrigerate for 1 to 2 hours.

Place on grill, cover with the hood or with foil. Allow to cook 40 minutes. At this point, shrimp should be tender enough to eat shell and all. Pour 1/4 cup dry sherry or white wine into shrimp packet. Serve shrimp hot. Makes 4 servings.

Boiled Shrimp with Sauces

2 quarts water	1 onion, quartered
Dash of hot sauce	1 celery heart
5 peppercorns	3 pounds fresh medium
1 lemon, sliced	shrimp
2 teaspoons salt	Garlic Mayonnaise (see Index)
1 clove garlic, peeled	
2 bay leaves	

Bring water to boil. Add hot sauce, peppercorns, lemon, salt, garlic, bay leaves, onion, and celery. Boil 10 minutes. Add shrimp. Bring water back to boil. Cook shrimp 6 to 8 minutes. Cover; remove from heat. Let stand 15 minutes; drain.

Peel and devein shrimp; chill.

Prepare sauce as directed in recipes.

Place shrimp on serving platter. Serve with sauce, large salad, and bread. Makes 6 servings or appetizers for 12.

Shrimp with Vegetables

2 (15-ounce) cans artichoke hearts	½ teaspoon dry mustard
1 small head cauliflower	1½ quarts water
1½ cups olive oil	5 peppercorns
½ cup vinegar	½ lemon, sliced
¼ cup dry white wine	1 bay leaf
1 tablespoon sugar	1 onion, peeled and quartered
1 teaspoon garlic juice	
4 teaspoons salt	1½ pounds fresh medium shrimp
Dash of cayenne	

Drain artichoke hearts.

Select saucepan large enough to accommodate head of cauliflower. Cover bottom of pan with 1 to 2 inches water. Add salt to water; bring to rapid boil. Add cauliflower to saucepan; cover. Cook 25 minutes or until fork-tender. Drain immediately; cool. Break into florets.

Combine oil, vinegar, wine, sugar, garlic juice, 2 teaspoons salt, cayenne, and mustard in jar. Cover; shake vigorously. Pour vinegar and oil mixture over vegetables. Cover; marinate in refrigerator overnight.

Bring water to boil. Add peppercorns, lemon, 2 teaspoons salt, bay leaf, and onion; boil 10 minutes. Add shrimp; bring water back to boil. Cook shrimp 6 to 8 minutes. Cover; remove from heat. Let stand 15 minutes; drain. Peel and devein shrimp; chill.

Add shrimp to marinating vegetables first thing in the morning. Recover. Return mixture to refrigerator; marinate at least 6 hours prior to serving. Drain before serving. Makes 6 to 8 servings.

Ranchero Corn

Lima Beans and Peppers

Escabeche of Sole

3 tablespoons butter	½ cup orange juice
¾ cup olive oil	Juice of 2 limes
Flour	¼ teaspoon Tabasco
6 small fillets sole	Orange slices
Salt and pepper	Lime slices
1 onion, thinly sliced and separated into rings	1 tablespoon orange zest (orange part of rind, grated or scraped)
1 green pepper, cut in thin rings	Chopped fresh cilantro
1 clove garlic, finely chopped	

Heat butter and 1/4 cup of oil. Flour fish fillets lightly and sauté them until delicately browned on both sides and just tender. Season to taste with salt and pepper.

Arrange fillets in a flat serving dish and top them with onion rings, pepper rings, and garlic Combine remaining 1/2 cup oil, orange juice, lime juice, Tabasco, and salt and pepper to taste. Blend well and pour over fish while it is still warm. Let stand in refrigerator 12 to 24 hours.

To serve, garnish with orange slices, lime slices, and orange zest. You may top with additional green pepper rings and chopped cilantro. Makes 6 servings.

Vegetables and Rice

Beans in Savory Sauce

1 **pound black beans (frijoles negroes)**	2 **pickled jalapeño peppers, seeded and finely chopped (Jalapeños en Escabeche)**
Water	1 **large tomato, peeled, seeded, and chopped**
2 **teaspoons salt**	1 **teaspoon crushed marjoram**
Savory Sauce	1 **teaspoon crushed oregano**
2 **tablespoons lard or olive oil**	**Salt and pepper to taste**
½ **cup onion, chopped**	**Chopped onions for topping**
1 **clove garlic, minced**	

Wash and pick over beans. Place in large saucepan; cover with water. Add salt; cook over low heat, replenishing water so that beans are always just covered. Cook at least 4 hours or until beans are very tender and mixture is thick.

Heat lard or oil in small skillet over moderate heat. Add onion and garlic; sauté until limp. Add peppers, tomato, herbs, and seasonings; reduce heat to simmer. Cook for 20 minutes. Add 1 cup beans and liquid to sauce; mash well. Add this mixture to pot of beans; cook 20 minutes more.

Serve beans hot in bowls; top with chopped onions. Makes 6 servings.

Note: If you have a slow cooker, the beans can be cooked in it all day. Be sure to add water occasionally so that they don't boil dry.

Steamed White Asparagus with Garlic Mayonnaise

2	pounds white asparagus	1	teaspoon salt
⅓	cup olive oil or butter		Garlic Mayonnaise (see Index)
⅔	cup water		

Break off each asparagus spear as far as it will snap easily; peel off scales with potato peeler. Rinse several times to remove sand.

Heat oil and water to boiling in pan large enough to accommodate asparagus stalks. Add asparagus and salt to boiling water; cover pan. Cook over high heat 12 minutes or until asparagus is fork-tender; drain. Serve asparagus immediately with Garlic Mayonnaise. Makes 6 servings.

Frijoles

2	cups pinto, black, or red kidney beans	3	tablespoons lard
2	onions, finely chopped		Salt and pepper to taste
2	cloves garlic, chopped	1	tomato, peeled, seeded, and chopped
	Sprig epazote or 1 bay leaf		
2	or more serrano chiles, chopped, or 1 teaspoon dried pequin chiles, crumbled		

Wash beans, but do not soak. Put in cold water to cover with 1/2 of the chopped onion and garlic, the epazote or bay leaf, and chiles. Cover and simmer gently, adding more hot water as needed. When beans begin to wrinkle, add 1 tablespoon lard or oil. When beans are soft and almost done, add seasonings. Cook another 1/2 hour without adding more water; there should not be a great deal of liquid when beans are done.

Heat remaining 2 tablespoons lard and sauté remaining chopped onion and garlic until limp. Add tomato and cook for 1 to 2 minutes; add a tablespoon of beans and mash into the mixture. Add a second tablespoon of beans without draining them so that some of the bean liquid evaporates in this cooking process.

Add a third tablespoon of beans and continue to cook until you have a smooth, fairly heavy paste. Return this to the bean pot and stir into beans over low heat to thicken the remaining liquid. Makes 6 to 8 servings.

Refried Beans: Cook beans as above, but when mashing them, keep adding beans until all have been mashed into lard over low heat. Add lard from time to time and cook until beans are creamy and have become a heavy, quite dry paste. You may use the blender to puree beans, adding them to the skillet bit by bit, and frying them dry in the hot lard.

Corn Casserole with Ham and Cheese

6 ears of corn (cut the corn off the cob)	3 eggs
3 or 4 slices ham	1⅔ to 2 cups sharp cheese, grated
1¼ cups milk	Pinch of nutmeg

Place corn and ham in a greased ovenproof pan.

Beat eggs and milk together. Add cheese and nutmeg. Pour this mixture over corn and ham. Bake at 400°F for 25 minutes. Makes 3 or 4 servings.

Ranchero Corn

6 slices bacon, diced	2 (12-ounce) cans vacuum-packed golden whole-kernel corn with sweet peppers, drained
1 (4½-ounce) jar sliced mushrooms, drained	
2 tablespoons onion, finely chopped	¾ cup Cheddar cheese, grated

Fry bacon in skillet over medium heat until cooked but not brown; drain off excess fat. Stir in mushrooms and onion; sauté until onion is tender. Blend in corn; heat through. Sprinkle with cheese; heat, without stirring, until cheese is melted. Makes 6 servings.

Green Beans in Tomato Sauce

3 tablespoons olive oil	1 tablespoon tomato paste
½ cup Spanish onion, chopped	½ teaspoon salt
	Dash of pepper
1 clove garlic, minced	1 teaspoon sugar
1 pound fresh green beans, washed and tips removed	1 tablespoon parsley
1 (16-ounce) can stewed tomatoes	

Heat oil in deep cast-iron skillet. Sauté onion and garlic until golden brown. Add remaining ingredients. Cover; cook 30 minutes or until beans are fork-tender. Remove beans.

Cook tomato sauce until almost all liquid evaporates. Re-add beans to sauce; reheat. Makes 6 servings.

Spanish Vegetables

Refried Black Beans

¼	pound bulk chorizo sausage	½	cup Queso Blanco or Jack cheese
¼	pound lard	½	cup onion, chopped
1	recipe Beans in Savory Sauce (see Index)		

Fry chorizo in large, heavy skillet until lightly browned. Add lard; melt it. Add beans slowly (a cup at a time) while mashing with potato masher to form a thick paste. Fry over low heat, stirring and mashing occasionally, until thick and crusty. Top with cheese; melt cheese.

Roll beans onto a platter and top with onion. Serve with tortillas or tostadas. Makes 6 servings.

Lima Beans and Peppers

1 (10-ounce) package frozen baby lima beans
3 tablespoons olive oil
½ cup green pepper, cut into thin strips
¼ cup sweet red pepper, cut into thin strips
¼ cup onion, finely chopped

Cook beans in boiling salted water, according to package directions. Drain; keep them warm.

Heat oil in small skillet. Add green pepper, red pepper, and onion; sauté for 5 minutes. Combine lima bean and pepper mixture gently. Serve immediately. Makes 4 servings.

Mexican Rice

3 tablespoons olive oil
1 cup raw long-grain rice
¼ cup green onions, chopped
¼ teaspoon garlic powder
2 cups chicken broth
3 tablespoons tomato paste
½ teaspoon ground cumin
¼ cup Jack cheese, grated
Chopped green onions for garnish

Heat oil in 2-quart saucepan over moderate heat. Add rice; sauté until very lightly browned. Add onions, garlic powder, and chicken broth; stir well. Stir in tomato paste and cumin. Bring mixture to a boil. Cover, reduce heat to low. Cook for 20 minutes or until all liquid is absorbed.

Place rice mixture in small ovenproof (preferably earthenware) casserole. Top with grated cheese. Bake in 350°F oven until cheese melts.

Garnish rice with green onions; serve. Makes 4 servings.

Saffron Rice

3 tablespoons olive oil
1 green pepper, chopped
1 red pepper, chopped
½ cup Spanish onion, chopped
1 cup long-grain rice
1 teaspoon garlic powder
⅛ teaspoon saffron
2 cups chicken broth

Heat oil in skillet. Add peppers and onion; sauté until wilted. Add rice; cook until opaque. Add remaining ingredients. Bring mixture to boil; cover. Reduce heat; simmer 30 minutes or until liquid is absorbed by rice. Makes 4 to 6 servings.

Spanish Crêpes

Spanish Vegetables

¾ cup split peas, plus water (1 teaspoon salt to 2 cups water) or 1 can (about 14 ounces) garbanzo beans
1 small eggplant (about 10 ounces) or an equal amount of squash
1 green pepper
1 red pepper
2 onions
1 tablespoon margarine or oil
1¼ cups chicken or beef broth
2 cloves garlic, crushed
1 teaspoon salt
1 teaspoon thyme
Pinch of ground saffron (optional)
4 hard-boiled eggs, halved
Coarse bread

Soak split peas in salted water 10 to 12 hours. Pour off water and boil in new lightly salted water 1 to 1-1/2 hours. Drain.

Slice eggplant or squash. Halve peppers, take out seeds and membranes, and cut them into strips.

Peel onions and chop into large pieces. Sauté onion in a little margarine. Add eggplant or squash and peppers. Add broth, garlic, salt, thyme, and saffron. Boil vegetables approximately 15 minutes until they become soft. Add more water if necessary. Stir in split peas; season to taste. Serve with hard-boiled egg halves and bread. Makes 4 servings.

Breads and Desserts

Corn Tortillas

2 cups instant Masa Harina	**1¼ cups water**
1 teaspoon salt	

Combine Masa and salt in mixing bowl. Make a well in center; stir in water. Dough must be stiff enough to hold together and not sticky. Add a little more water if necessary. Knead dough until pliable. Form into a 12-inch log; cut into 1-inch pieces. Roll pieces into balls; cover with a damp cloth while shaping tortillas.

Shaping with a tortilla press: Place dough between 2 polyethylene bags, center on the press, and flatten. Carefully peel off plastic bags; stack tortillas between sheets of waxed paper until all are ready to cook.

Without a tortilla press: Place dough ball between sheets of waxed paper; flatten with heavy skillet or large pie plate, or use a rolling pin. Turn tortilla to keep it round as you roll. Tortillas should be 6 inches in diameter and quite thin.

Heat a griddle or cast-iron skillet (ungreased) until quite hot. Peel waxed paper off top of tortilla; place it on griddle. Wait several seconds, then gently peel waxed paper off other side of tortilla as the first side cooks on the griddle. Bake until lightly flecked with brown (about 2 minutes). Turn; cook 1 minute more. Stack, wrap in foil, and keep tortillas warm in oven. Makes 12, 6-inch tortillas.

Flour Tortillas

3 **cups all-purpose flour**	½ **teaspoon salt**
¼ **cup cold lard or**	1 **cup water**
hydrogenated shortening,	
cut into 4 pieces	

Place flour, shortening, and salt in processor bowl. Process with metal blade until consistency of cornmeal. Add water and process until a ball forms on the blades or the motor begins to stall, about 5 seconds.

Knead dough on a floured surface for 3 to 4 minutes. Cover and let rest for 20 to 30 minutes. Divide dough into 10 balls. Roll out each between 2 sheets of waxed paper to a 7-inch circle. Peel off top sheet and invert into a preheated, ungreased frying pan. Heat, peel off top paper; turn when lightly browned and brown the other side.

Serve at once or wrap in aluminum foil and refrigerate. Rewarm package in a 250°F oven for 4 to 5 minutes. Makes 10, 7-inch tortillas.

King's Bread Ring

2 **packages active dry yeast**	***Rum Icing***
1 **cup warm milk**	1⅓ **cups powdered sugar**
⅓ **cup sugar**	1 **to 2 tablespoons milk**
⅓ **cup margarine**	1 **teaspoon rum flavoring**
2 **teaspoons salt**	
1½ **teaspoons orange peel,**	***Candied-Fruit Topping***
freshly grated	5 **candied cherries, chopped**
3 **eggs, well beaten**	10 **candied orange peel strips**
4 **to** 4½ **cups all-purpose flour**	
¼ **cup margarine, melted**	

Sprinkle yeast on milk; stir to dissolve. Cream sugar and 1/3 cup margarine. Blend in salt and orange peel. Add 1 egg, yeast mixture, and enough flour to make stiff dough. Turn out on lightly floured surface; knead until smooth and elastic, about 10 minutes. Place in greased bowl; grease top. Cover; let rise until double in bulk. Punch down.

Knead until smooth, about 2 minutes. Roll dough into long rope; place on greased cookie sheet. Shape into ring, sealing ends together. Push a coin into dough so it is completely covered. Brush with 1/4 cup margarine. Cover; let rise until double in bulk, about 1-1/2 hours. Bake at 375°F 30 minutes or until golden brown; cool.

Combine powdered sugar, milk, and rum flavoring. Beat until smooth. Frost bread with icing; decorate with candied fruit as illustrated. Makes 12 servings.

Puffed Bread

4	**cups flour**	¼	**cup shortening**
4	**teaspoons baking powder**		**1 to 1½ cups water, as needed**
2	**teaspoons salt**		**Oil for frying**

Sift dry ingredients into mixing bowl. Cut in shortening. Add water, a little at a time, stirring to form a stiff dough. Knead until smooth. Roll thin; cut into 2-inch squares or triangles.

Heat oil in deep, heavy pan to 365°F; deep-fry dough pieces a few at a time until golden brown. They will puff up as they fry. Serve hot with butter and jelly or honey. Makes about 40.

Mocha Cherry and Nut Cookies

1	**cup butter**	½	**teaspoon salt**
½	**cup sugar**	1	**cup pecans, finely**
2	**teaspoons vanilla**		**chopped**
2	**cups flour, sifted**	½	**cup maraschino cherries,**
¼	**cup unsweetened cocoa**		**chopped**
1	**tablespoon instant coffee**	1	**box confectioners' sugar**

Cream butter, sugar, and vanilla until fluffy. Sift flour, cocoa, instant coffee, and salt together. Gradually add dry ingredients to creamed mixture. Add pecans and cherries. Chill dough.

Shape dough into balls, using 1 generous teaspoon of dough for each ball. Place on greased cookie sheets. Bake in 325°F oven 20 minutes. Remove from cookie sheets to cooling racks. While warm, sprinkle with confectioners' sugar. Makes 6 dozen.

Mexican Wedding Cakes

1	**cup butter or margarine**	½	**teaspoon salt**
⅓	**cup sugar**	1	**cup Brazil nuts, finely**
1	**teaspoon almond flavoring**		**chopped**
	2½ cups flour, sifted		**Red and green food coloring**

Work butter and sugar in a bowl until creamy. Stir in flavoring. Stir in flour, salt, and nuts; mix thoroughly. Divide dough in half. Stir a few drops of red coloring into one half; green coloring into the other. Chill several hours.

Form into 1-inch balls. Place on greased baking sheets. Cover bottom of a glass with damp cheesecloth and use it to flatten each ball to 1/4-inch thickness. Bake in a 325°F oven 12 to 15 minutes or until the cookies start to brown a little around the edges. Makes about 3 dozen.

Spanish Crêpes

4 eggs	3 tablespoons kirsch
1 cup flour	2 tablespoons Grand Marnier
2 tablespoons sugar	1 cup sour cream
1 cup milk	8 ounces cream cheese, softened
¼ cup water	½ cup sugar
1 tablespoon margarine, melted	Powdered sugar for dusting
8 Valencia oranges	

Beat eggs with whisk in medium mixing bowl. Gradually add flour and sugar alternately with milk and water, beating until smooth. Beat in margarine. Refrigerate 1 hour before using.

Prepare crêpes.

Peel oranges. Cut into segments, cutting between membranes. Slice each segment into 3 to 4 pieces. Sprinkle oranges with kirsch and Grand Marnier.

Blend sour cream, cream cheese, and sugar. Fold oranges into cream mixture, saving 1/2 cup for garnish. Top each crêpe with 2 to 3 tablespoons cheese and orange mixture. Roll up. Place crêpes on serving platter. Dust with powdered sugar. Garnish with orange slices. Makes 6 servings.

Cinnamon Flan

1 cup sugar	1 cup water
2 tablespoons water	½ teaspoon cinnamon
4 eggs	½ teaspoon lemon rind, grated
1 (14-ounce) can sweetened condensed milk	

Combine sugar and 2 tablespoons water in heavy, small skillet. Cook, stirring constantly, until caramelized and syrupy. Immediately pour into warm, 4-cup, buttered mold; tilt to coat bottom and sides of container while sugar is still hot.

Beat eggs well. Add milk, 1 cup water, cinnamon, and lemon peel; mix well. Pour into prepared mold. Place casserole in larger pan containing hot water to level of custard. Bake at 350°F 1 hour or until knife inserted in center comes out clean. Cool completely.

Loosen custard with knife; invert on serving platter. Spoon caramel over top. Makes 4 to 6 servings.

Traditional Fried Crullers

Traditional Fried Crullers

Oil for deep frying
½ lime
1   cup water
**1   (10-ounce) package pie-
       crust mix**

3   eggs
Powdered sugar

Heat oil to 370°F in large, heavy skillet. Oil should be 3 inches deep and pan no more than half full. Add lime.

Bring water to boil. Quickly stir in pie-crust mix; stir until mixture forms ball and leaves sides of pan. Transfer dough to pastry bag fitted with star tip.

Remove lime from fat. Squeeze dough into hot fat in continuous spiral to fill pan. Do not crowd. Cook until golden brown, turning once during cooking process; drain. Dust with powdered sugar. Serve immediately. Makes 6 servings.

Sweet Fritters

4¾ cups flour
½ cup sugar
¼ teaspoon salt
1 cup water
2 eggs
3 tablespoons rum

Oil for frying
1 teaspoon ground cinnamon
½ cup sugar

Sift flour, sugar, and salt together into large bowl. Beat water, eggs, and rum together. Pour into flour mixture; mix to form a stiff dough. Turn out on floured board; knead for 2 minutes or until smooth. Cut into 4 pieces. Roll each piece on floured pastry cloth to a rectangle (10 × 15 inches); cut into strips (2 × 5 inches). Shape by twisting 2 strips together, or cut a 1-inch slit down center of strip and pull 1 end through slit.

Heat oil to 370°F in an electric skillet. Meanwhile, combine cinnamon and sugar in shallow pan. Deep-fry pastries until golden. Drain briefly, dip in cinnamon sugar, and coat well. Makes 40.

Mexican Trifle

¼ cup sugar
1 tablespoon cornstarch
¼ teaspoon salt
2 cups milk
2 eggs, slightly beaten
1 teaspoon vanilla
4 cups pound cake, cubed
4 tablespoons brandy

4 tablespoons apricot preserves
½ cup whipped cream
1 tablespoon confectioners' sugar
Grated semisweet chocolate
Toasted slivered almonds

Combine sugar, cornstarch, and salt in medium saucepan. Stir in milk until well blended. Cook over medium heat, stirring constantly, until mixture boils (it will be quite thin). Add a little custard to beaten eggs; beat well. Return to saucepan; cook, stirring constantly, until mixture starts to bubble. Stir in vanilla; cool, covered with waxed paper.

Place cake cubes in glass bowl. Sprinkle with 3 tablespoons of brandy and drizzle with preserves. Pour custard over cake cubes. Whip cream with confectioners' sugar until stiff. Fold in 1 tablespoon brandy.

Top cake and custard with whipped cream. Garnish with grated chocolate and almonds. Cover and chill for several hours before serving. Makes 4 to 6 servings.

Saffron Advent Cake

Saffron Advent Cake

2 cups flour	1/8 to 1/4 teaspoon saffron, ground
3 teaspoons baking powder	Butter and bread crumbs or flour for preparing the pan
3/4 cup sugar	
7 tablespoons butter or margarine	3 or 4 apples, thinly sliced
2/3 cup milk	A little sugar and several dabs of butter
1 egg	

Blend flour, baking powder, and sugar. Crumble butter into mixture until it is grainy.

Beat milk, egg, and saffron together. Pour into flour mixture. Quickly work together into a dough. Place dough in a greased baking pan, preferably with a detachable edge (springform), which has been dusted with bread crumbs or flour. Stick thin slices of apples close together into the dough. Sprinkle with a little sugar. Place several dabs of butter on top. Bake in a 425°F oven for 25 to 30 minutes. Makes 10 servings.

Hot Chocolate Mexican-Style

Mexican Cinnamon Tea Cakes

1	cup butter	¼	teaspoon salt
1½	cups sugar	1	teaspoon baking powder
2	eggs	2	tablespoons sugar
2¾	cups flour	2	teaspoons cinnamon
1	teaspoon cream of tartar		

Cream butter and 1-1/2 cups sugar. Add eggs. Sift dry ingredients; add to egg mixture. Shape dough into small balls, using approximately 1 teaspoon dough for each cookie.

Roll balls in mixture of 2 tablespoons sugar and 2 teaspoons cinnamon. Flatten slightly. Place on greased cookie sheet. Bake for 8 to 10 minutes at 400°F. Remove from cookie sheet and cool on a rack. Makes 4 dozen.

Hot Chocolate Mexican-Style

2 **(1-ounce) squares unsweetened chocolate**	2 **cups milk**
½ **teaspoon vanilla**	2 **egg yolks**
1 **teaspoon ground cinnamon**	2 **tablespoons sugar**
	3 **ounces brandy**
4 **tablespoons heavy cream**	4 **cinnamon sticks**

In a saucepan, combine chocolate, vanilla, cinnamon, and cream; place over very low heat, stirring until chocolate is melted. Add milk slowly to chocolate mixture; mix well. Warm over very low heat. Do not allow mixture to boil.

Beat egg yolks and sugar until foamy. Slowly pour part of chocolate mixture into egg yolks, beating well. Pour egg-yolk mixture back into saucepan; beat. Add brandy to chocolate mixture; beat until mixture is frothy. Serve hot chocolate immediately in small cups with cinnamon sticks used as stirrers. Makes 4 servings.

Note: A simpler method for making delicious chocolate is as follows: For each cup of chocolate, heat 1 cup milk until quite hot (do not boil). Pour over 1 ounce (per cup of milk) of grated Mexican chocolate; stir until melted. Whip with a rotary beater until frothy, and serve. If Mexican chocolate is unavailable, substitute 1 ounce of unsweetened chocolate, grated, and 1/4 teaspoon ground cinnamon for each ounce of Mexican chocolate.

EQUIVALENT MEASURES

dash = 2 or 3 drops
pinch = amount that can be held
          between ends of thumb &
          forefinger
1 tablespoon = 3 teaspoons
¼ cup = 4 tablespoons
⅓ cup = 5 tablespoons + 1 teaspoon
½ cup = 8 tablespoons
1 cup = 16 tablespoons
1 pint = 2 cups
1 quart = 4 cups
1 gallon = 4 quarts
1 peck = 8 quarts
1 bushel = 4 pecks
1 pound = 16 ounces

KITCHEN METRIC

measurements you will encounter
most often in recipes are: centimeter
(cm), milliliter (ml), gram (g),
kilogram (kg)

cup equivalents (volume):

    ¼   cup = 60 ml
    ⅓   cup = 85 ml
    ½   cup = 125 ml
    ⅔   cup = 170 ml
    ¾   cup = 180 ml
    1   cup = 250 ml
    1¼   cups = 310 ml
    1½   cups = 375 ml
    2   cups = 500 ml
    3   cups = 750 ml
    5   cups = 1250 ml

spoonful equivalents (volume):

    ⅛   teaspoon = .5 ml
    ¼   teaspoon = 1.5 ml
    ½   teaspoon = 3 ml
    ¾   teaspoon = 4 ml
    1   teaspoon = 5 ml
    1   tablespoon = 15 ml
    2   tablespoons = 30 ml
    3   tablespoons = 45 ml

pan sizes (linear & volume):

    1 inch = 2.5 cm
    8-inch square = 20-cm square
    9 × 13 × 1½-inch = 20 × 33 × 4-cm

10 × 6 × 2-inch = 25 × 15 × 5-cm
13 × 9 × 2-inch = 33 × 23 × 5-cm
7½ × 12 × 1½-inch = 18 × 30 × 4-cm
  (above are baking dishes, pans)
9 × 5 × 3-inch = 23 × 13 × 8-cm
  (loaf pan)
10-inch = 25 cm   12-inch = 30-cm
  (skillets)
1-quart = 1-liter   2-quart = 2-liter
  (baking dishes, by volume)
5- to 6-cup = 1.5-liter
  (ring mold)

weight (meat amounts;
  can & package sizes):

    1   ounce = 28 g
    ½   pound = 225 g
    ¾   pound = 340 g
    1   pound = 450 g
    1½   pounds = 675 g
    2   pounds = 900 g
    3   pounds = 1.4 kg (in recipes,
           amounts of meat above 2 pounds
           will generally be stated in
           kilograms)
    10   ounces = 280 g
           (most frozen vegetables)
    10½   ounces = 294 g
           (most condensed soups)
    15   ounces = 425 g
           (common can size)
    16   ounces = 450 g
           (common can size)
    1   pound, 24 ounces = 850 g
           (can size)

OVEN TEMPERATURES

275°F = 135°C
300°F = 149°C
325°F = 165°C
350°F = 175°C
375°F = 190°C
400°F = 205°C
425°F = 218°C
450°F = 230°C
500°F = 260°C

Note that Celsius temperatures are
sometimes rounded off to the nearest
reading ending in 0 or 5; the Celsius
thermometer is the same as
Centigrade, a term no longer used.

Index

Recipe photograph page number in italic.